AF235259

THE
JOWETTS
THAT GOT AWAY

THE
JOWETTS
THAT GOT AWAY

NOEL STOKOE

FONTHILL

Fonthill Media Language Policy

Fonthill Media publishes in the international English language market. One language edition is published worldwide. As there are minor differences in spelling and presentation, especially with regard to American English and British English, a policy is necessary to define which form of English to use. The Fonthill Policy is to use the form of English native to the author. Noel Stokoe was born and educated in York and now lives in Whitby, North Yorkshire; therefore, British English has been adopted in this publication.

Fonthill Media Limited
Fonthill Media LLC
www.fonthillmedia.com
office@fonthillmedia.com

First published in the United Kingdom and the United States of America 2022

British Library Cataloguing in Publication Data:
A catalogue record for this book is available from the British Library

Copyright © Noel Stokoe 2022

ISBN 978-1-78155-862-1

The right of Noel Stokoe to be identified as the author of this work has been asserted by him in accordance with the Copyright, Designs and Patents Act 1988.

All rights reserved. No part of this publication may be reproduced, stored in a retrieval system or transmitted in any form or by any means, electronic, mechanical, photocopying, recording or otherwise, without prior permission in writing from Fonthill Media Limited

Typeset in 10pt on 13pt MinionPro
Printed and bound in England

CONTENTS

INTRODUCTION

THE HISTORY OF Jowett Cars is well-documented already, but in a nutshell, they were built in Bradford from 1906 to 1954. The Jowett Company was formed by brothers Ben and William Jowett and was Yorkshire's only mass-produced car. All pre-war cars up to 1935 were powered by a twin-cylinder horizontally opposed 7-hp engine known as 'the little engine with the big pull'. In 1935, a new four-cylinder horizontally opposed engine was introduced with a 10-hp rating running alongside the original twin-cylinder model, which had been increased to an 8-hp rating. There were several attempts at new models during this period, several of which were made in very limited numbers, where sadly, there are no survivors today.

The most notable departure came about in 1933 where experiments with a four-cylinder inline engine, which was at odds with long-established Jowett principles of 'flat' engines, so much so, it was badged as a La Roche to avoid loyal Yorkshire buyers panicking at the thought of the flat-twin engine being done away with—us Yorkshire folk do not like changes. They need not have worried as only two were built due to the performance being disappointing, so the project was abandoned.

During the late 1930s, there were massive changes in the Jowett company. It was floated on the stock exchange in 1935, much against Ben's wishes. William also retired at the outbreak of war in 1939 with both Jowett brothers retiring, meaning there was now no family involvement with the company. During the war, the company switched to producing armaments for the war effort.

The first all-new model was the Javelin saloon, launched in 1947; this was the brainchild of Gerald Palmer, who was recruited by Jowetts in 1942 from the Nuffield Group to design an all-new post-war model. This was a massive departure for Jowetts and took the motoring press by storm; it has long been regarded as Britain's first all-new post-war car.

This in turn led to the development of the Jupiter sportscar, which was launched in 1950. This model won its class at Le Mans in 1950, 1951, and again in 1952 in a much-lightened model known as the R1. In 1953, a new Jupiter known as the R4 was launched just in time for the Motor Show, which was hoped would save the ailing company, but sadly, it was not to be with only three prototypes being built.

As early as 1951, there should have been a completely new range of cars, vans, pick-up and estate cars known as the Bradford CD range. Due to financial constraints and problems with

Briggs, the producer of Javelin and Bradford van bodies, they never reached production with only approximately fifteen prototypes being built. There was even talk of upgrading the Javelin and Jupiter engine from a 1½ litres to 2½ litres, but unfortunately this never materialised. A six-cylinder inline engine was also being considered, codenamed the Venus, but sadly, this was another idea that got no further than the technical drawing stage, with one engine only partially built at the time of the closure of the factory.

Sadly, the new Jupiter R4 sports car and the CD Bradford range never made it into production in a very rapidly changing market, where only the larger manufacturers survived.

At least Jowetts went out of production in a blaze of glory, rather than becoming yet another badge-engineered make like Riley, Wolseley, and so many more. The history of Jowetts could have been so very different had fate been kinder to them in those early post-war years.

Noel Stokoe, February 2022

1

1926
JACKSON JOWETT

JACKSONS OF CROYDON were coachbuilders at Mobile House, Park Street, Croydon. The company had three directors—W. T. S. Jackson, W. H. O. Jackson, and A. Edward. They took a standard long-wheelbase Jowett chassis and fitted a sporting two-seater body of their own design.

The covering letter, with a sales booklet, which was sent out to a potential purchaser in November 1926, read as follows:

Dear Sir, we thank you for your esteemed enquiry, and as requested, enclose catalogue of our Sports Tourer:—

The Jackson Jowett can never be appreciated by merely a catalogue—it is a car with performance and appearance equal to others marketed at £300 and over. Our years and years of studied application to the Jowett and its capabilities have resulted in a car 'par excellence.'

In guaranteeing the speeds as minimum we again refer to our policy of satisfaction—an owner is all the more pleased to better the maker's specification than to complain that it was overstated. The Jackson Jowett has attained a speed of 48mph in second and 60mph in top so on this score we are sure of your satisfaction.

Colours may be had on your own choice without extra charge—standard colours are Royal Blue body and wheels, Cherry Red beading, wings and valances, hubs black. Hair carpet bound leather and fitted leather heel pad standard.

The backs of the seats are adjustable (front and rear) and a special study has been made of the body position in driving. Absolute support to all vital parts has been given to ensure extreme comfort for any length of journey.

If further advice or particulars will assist you, may we ask the favour of your commands?

With the assurance of our personal and prompt attention.

We are, dear Sir,

Yours faithfully,

Jackson's of Croydon Ltd.

To this end, the sales brochure entitled *The De-luxe of Tourers—The Jackson Jowett* goes on to say:

The name Jowett is now so well known—worldwide—that with little ado we commend the reader to study the achievements of the Jowett car since its introduction in 1910, through years of successful history making in the motor world.

The Jowett will, and has, accomplished journeys which no other car has, and seemingly, will—there remains a challenge to the motoring world. Just read about it in the booklet 'Across Africa in 60 days.' Frankly, knowing the Jowett as we do, that challenge is likely to remain unaccepted.

If you need assurance of the satisfaction of the Jowett owner, stop one, anyone, and ask—there never was a dissatisfied owner; they all brim over with praise for the car, and admit astonishment at its capabilities.

Perchance, and you are a motorist, you have had a Jowett pass you on a hill and watched its progress without power of redress for the seeming impudence of a 7hp car—but quite honestly it has amazed you.

That's just it—the Jowett is an amazing car.

The owner-driver who appreciates a car with a good turn of speed, quick acceleration, and a sporty kick in the engine, does not necessarily appreciate spending hours with his head under the bonnet, or pounds and pounds in an endeavour to retain that beloved 'tune.'

Also, there is little pleasure if the exhilaration of a fast car has to be enjoyed on a glorified 'buck board.' Our aim has been to produce a sports touring car without sacrificing reliability or comfort.

The Jackson Jowett will run all day with the throttle wide open without stress or fuss, with the unfailing reliability characteristic of the Jowett, and in such comfort as only the 'divan' seats can give – you enjoy the restfulness of your favourite arm chair in the Jackson Jowett at speed.

The orthodox 'dicky seat' with its discomfort and ugliness, has been replaced with the same comfortable seat as fitted to the front; you have a real 2-seater or full 4-seater at will, but with all the pleasing lines of a streamlined 2-seater.

We conceived that the car which would accomplish long journeys at high speeds at high average speeds, without the necessity of dirty hands and clothes, fatigue or cramp, would mean luxury to you and your friends.

No contortions become necessary to get at the controls—your body position remains unchanged. Ideal for Town work or Touring.

The front seats are stuffed with 'curled hair' and covered in antique-grain real leather, which allows you to enjoy the restfulness of your favourite armchair in the Jackson Jowett at speed. The car has a quick acceleration and a sporty kick in the engine and a good turn of speed.

Specification

Engine, RAC rating 7hp, 2-cylinder horizontally opposed, water cooled. Bore2.31/32inches (75.4mm). Stroke 4inches (101.5mm). Capacity 907.2 cc.

Pistons are made of aluminium with three rings, connecting rods machined for lightness, and inlet and exhaust passages smoothed allowing easy passage for gases. Develops considerably more than the usual Jowett bhp—already a renowned feature—being specially tuned for speed and power.

Chassis—Standard Jowett (long 2-seater)

Lubrication, chassis lubrication, cooling, gearbox, front axle, rear axle, carburettor, ignition, lighting, starting, clutch, brakes, steering gear, and petrol system – all standard Jowett.

Suspension – standard Jowett, fitted B & D stabilisers front and rear.

Wheels and tyres, Lynton Disc or Dunlop Artillery, Dunlop reinforced balloon tyres, 27 × 4.40.

Instrument Board—covered grained leather.

Windscreen—sports type, fitted best plate glass, opening at top.

Bodywork—body is framed up in well-seasoned English ash, panelled in aluminium and hand enamelled.

Upholstery—Curled hair stuffed seats and squabs, covered in real leather, antique grain – red.

Hood—One man type, fixing to the top of the screen with rigid side curtains.

Equipment —B & D Stabilisers front and rear. Two large size head lamps, two side lamps and a tail lamp. Two dash lamps, Speedometer, Electric Horn, Smith automatic screen wiper, Driving Mirror, Oil tell tale.

Air strangler, Lucas switchboard, Spare wheel, Grease gun, Full set of tools and tool roll, Canister oil container fixed under bonnet, Dynamo starting and lighting set, Oil can, Dip stick, Wheel brace, Jack and Pump.

Speed and comfort—Reliability with Economy—Price at Works … £187 10*s*

Worthy of consideration:—

Tax £7.00 per annum

Petrol Consumption 45mpg

Oil Consumption 1,500mpg

Tyre Mileage 15,000 miles per set

Speeds – Guaranteed Minimum

First Gear 25mph

Second Gear 40mph

Third Gear 50mph

A 2-seater of such pleasing lines and comfort as are only associated with high priced cars. 'Pullman car' travel at less than '3rd Class' fare for one.

It is hills where your 'average' goes. You cease to envy the other fellow with a high-powered and priced car—a smile at the thought of your Tax and Petrol bill—and pass by!

Our enthusiasm in the Jowett is such that having produced a special Sports model you will more readily appreciate our ability to offer you first class service if your requirements are for the ordinary touring models.

What others say:

Gentlemen, 'The car has now done more than 1,500 miles, and is an absolute gem, and £100 cheaper than a new ----, and is, as far as my experience goes, very much more reliable. Nothing whatsoever has gone wrong in the slightest particular. I am intensely satisfied. She did 270 miles in a day the other Saturday and 300 miles this Whitsun and was a dream the whole time. Motoring now is an inexpensive pleasure…I would supplement my remarks by stating that the satisfaction in the car is only excelled by your service and courtesy and attention to the minutest requests.'

Yours faithfully, L C Appleton, 103 Melfont Road, Thornton Heath.

Sadly, there are no Jackson Jowett survivors today.

The front cover of the rather lavish sales booklet for the Jackson Jowett. Sadly, very few of these cars appear to have been built and none survive today.

Disc wheels, the V-shaped screen and copper exhaust pipe are items which have received attention in the conversion.

(Above) The long bonnet, sloping wings and tapering tail give an appearance of speed to this Jackson Jowett.

A snippet from one of the period motoring magazines referred to the long bonnet, sloping wings, and tapering tail that gave the appearance of speed. The V-shaped screen and copper exhaust pipe were also features of this model.

The Jackson Jowett was produced in 1926. Jacksons of Croydon was a garage and coachbuilder at Mobile House, Park Street, Croydon; their letterheads said the premises were 'opposite the General Post Office' building.

I sent this picture to *The Jowetteer* magazine, which was published on the back cover of the April 1989 issue. It was identified by club member Robert Baines at that time: 'The photo was taken in Holstead, Colchester in about 1936. It shows John Frost at the wheel, who was still living at the old windmill outside of which the photo was taken. He told me it was one of 12 Jackson Jowett cars built in the mid-1920s. The car was bought second hand for £14 and was run by Mr Frost during the 1930s'. He also said that 'the car was yellow and red, and noisy!'

2

1926
WAIT & SEE

I N TRUTH, I would not really class the 'Wait & See' cars as prototype models as they were in fact a special order that had been requested by Frank Gray, the ex-MP for Oxford in 1926. He had argued that the British motor industry was not producing cars for colonial use.

He challenged them to provide him with cars that would be capable of crossing Africa, which would involve them carrying all their own petrol, water, and provisions, as most of the journey would have to be covered without any outside help. There were virtually no roads or services in Africa at that time. Needless to say, there were no offers forthcoming from other car manufacturers, as such a trip had never been attempted before. The Jowett brothers, however, realised the free advertising potential such a trip would create and agreed to sell Gray two cars. Being two shrewd Yorkshiremen, they said they would repay Gray the cost of the two cars if the trip was successful; this way, the brothers thought that Gray would also have a financial interest in completing the challenge.

Gray would drive one car and Jack Sawyer, a wealthy neighbour of Gray, would drive the other. It should be noted that Sawyer could not drive but would learn on the trip. Sawyer travelled to the Jowett factory and chose two long chassis two-seaters and asked for a lorry flat-back rather than the dickey seat. He also required tow bars fitting to the cars, as they would both have to tow trailers loaded with provisions. At a press conference prior to the cars' departure for Africa, a reporter asked Ben Jowett if the cars had any real chance of completing such an arduous journey; he replied, 'wait and see'. Gladney Haigh, Jowett's publicity man, heard this and ordered the two cars to have written on each side one with 'Wait' and the other 'See'. Ever since then, these cars have been known as the Wait & See cars.

The crossing was to be from Lagos in the west to Massawa in the east. Most of the route would be across open country and desert as there were few roads of any kind. While in Lagos, Gray and Sawyer enlisted the help of two locals, one as a cook and Bismark as the mechanic. Bismark agreed to make the crossing, provided that they would take him to England for an extended holiday afterwards; Gray and Sawyer agreed to this request. Prior to the start of journey, the local dignitaries invited them to dinner, none of whom gave them a chance of success.

The expedition set off from Lagos on 16 March, going was good and they covered almost 300 miles in the first two days. They reached Kano to meet up with the trailers that had been sent ahead of them; these were loaded with petrol, water, tyres, and provisions. They would now be on their own for the next 1,600 miles of mainly desert until they reached El-Obeid. During this part of the journey, the terrain was very difficult, and they were lucky to cover 100 miles per fourteen-hour day. The heat was so great that the cars' bodywork could not be touched during the day without causing burns. There were various problems *en route*, but neither car had any major mechanical problems, and the expedition reached Massawa sixty days later on 14 May, which represented only forty-nine driving days, as eleven days were rest days. In all, a total of 3,800 miles were covered; they even had time to rescue a slave girl and transport her 120 miles with them to a district judge and safety.

Needless to say, the press loved this story of British endeavour, and Jowett Cars received vast amounts of publicity. Gray and Sawyer were true to their word and brought Bismark back to England with them. Bismark and the two cars went on tour, calling at Jowett agents to allow the cars to be inspected this also generated a great deal of publicity in local papers. The cars were later used as factory transport at Jowetts for several years delivering spare parts to agents. Later, they were used by the Artillery Transport Company, based in York. Sadly, their fate is unknown.

Luckily, an exact replica of *See* has been constructed in recent years, including a replica of the Eccles trailer that the two cars towed on this epic journey. I know I have already detailed this story in much more detail in two of my previous books, *Sporting Jowetts* and *Jowetts of the 1920s*, but it is such a great story I could not resist retelling it again—it would make a great film.

The 'Wait & See' cars at the Jowett works prior to the crossing of Africa in 1926, driven by the former Oxford MP Frank Gray and his friend, Jack Sawyer.

The 'Wait & See' cars arrived back to the UK in triumph after the crossing of Africa. This is See; the person in the passenger seat is Bismark, the African mechanic hired by Gray. He agreed to the trip provided that they would bring him over to the UK for an extended holiday after the trip, which Gray agreed to.

3

1928
JOWETT SPORTS

I N THE EARLY 1920s, car manufacturers were looking for ways to extol the virtues of their products, and a very popular way to do this was enter their cars in trials and freak hill-climbs. Both Ben and William Jowett entered and drove their cars in events, such as the Scottish 1,000-mile six-day trial. Major L. D. Johnstone also competed in these events in 1921 and 1922 in a Jowett two-seater registered AK9129 with considerable success.

He approached the Jowett brothers to have a car built to his own specification, to suit the requirements of trials work. The major took delivery of the new car, registered KU1926, on 26 April 1923, and on 7 May, he took part in the Scottish 1,000-mile six-day trial. On this occasion, he was the only Jowett entrant and was awarded with a gold award for his efforts. He also took part in the London–Edinburgh run later that month and in the Land's End–London trial in 1924.

The major continued using the car in events but sold it to Bob Grant of Dumfries in November 1926, who raced and rallied the car for almost fifty years, apart from nine years between 1955 and 1964 when it was on loan to the Sword Collection in Kilmarnock.

Various upgrades were made to the car over the years to keep it competitive which included fitting 1929-style wings and wheels sometime in the 1930s. There are many fittings on the car that are not standard for a 1923 model but were so on this particular car.

Bob Grant died in 1991 aged ninety-six, and the car was passed on to his son Harris in accordance with Jowett's old advertising slogan: 'Jowetts never wear out—they are left to your next of kin!' Sadly, Harris also died in 1998, and after lengthy negotiations, the car was sold in 2002 to Mike Koch-Osborne, who is very well known in Jowett circles as he is the grandson of William Jowett.

The car has been used extensively by Mike since then and has appeared at many of the Jowett Car Club international rallies and events.

Following the success of this car, it led to other sports models being built by the factory. One was built for Victoria Worsley, who raced it extensively in 1928 and 1929 at Brooklands and in the early reliability trials and grass track races.

Another (possibly a Jackson Jowett; see earlier chapter) was loaned to J. J. Hall, a professional record-breaker who was based at Brooklands. The car was built at the Jowett works to attempt to break the twelve-hour Class G record at Brooklands. His co-driver was Horace Grimley, who was in charge of Jowett's Experimental Department. They were successful in their attempt (just) as they had to replace no fewer than three cylinder head gaskets during the twelve hours, plus remove a swarm of bees that got into the radiator grill and caused overheating. This record was never broken before Brooklands closed down in 1939 due to the Second World War, so this record still stands as the Brooklands track never re-opened after the war.

Following these successes, the Jowett brothers thought it would be a good idea to produce a sports model in the hope it would appeal to 'sporting lads and lasses', but unfortunately, it did not.

There was a full-page advert for the 'New Sports Model' published in *The Motor* on 11 October 1927 under the heading 'Another Triumph':

Youth will be served. The 'lads' of the high road with their nerve and skill were bound to look for an edition of the Jowett two-seater which would fly the banner of youth. Also, the 'lasses' who sport the beret. Well, they will cheer when they see it. It's as slick and trim and 'dare devil' as a submarine chaser. Look at the lovely wave-line that gives her a clean clipper air. And the low-slung body, lying back from the front wheels as if perfectly poised for a dive.

Without a doubt the Jowett secret of leg roominess has a pull here. For the sporting motorist can stretch his legs and lie back at the authentic angle in a most nonchalant angle. The outside handbrake and gear lever give a business-like too, and get down to business in a tight corner.

The new Sports Model will set up a sensation with the rising generation. In it the little engine with the big pull is out to achieve new conquests. She'll go to the limit and then some.

All the Jowett ingenuity is here exercised to the last point, a car as lean and keen as a winning greyhound—a thing of speed and beauty that is a joy to its owner. It is guaranteed to do 60mph.

See our Stand number 125 at Olympia—Price £145.00.

The car was also described in the 1928 sales booklet in a similar fashion:

Another Triumph—The New 'Sports' £145 (ex-works)—Guaranteed to do 60 miles per hour.

Youth will be served. The 'lads' of nerve and skill looked for an edition of the Jowett two-seater which would fly.

They will cheer when they see it; as slick and trim and 'dare devil' as a submarine chaser, with its low-slung body.

Leg-roominess has a pull here. The outside hand brake and gear lever handy in a tight corner.

All the Jowett ingenuity is here exercised to the last point—a car of speed and beauty.

The Jowett Sports was not the only new model to be announced in 1928; there was also the Jowett Coupé. Both of these models were described in *The Motor* and *The Autocar* in September 1927, so I am only quoting the part relating to the Sports model.

The Autocar 23 September 1927: Sports and Coupé Jowetts

Two Additions to the Range of the Well-Known 7-hp Two-Cylinder Car

For many years the Jowett chassis has been produced along the same lines, the makers adhering to a policy of continuity of one type which undoubtedly has had much to do with their success and with the confidence created in their cars….

The second new model is perhaps a more unexpected innovation for the Jowett. This is a sports two-seater of a very racy appearance.

By setting the engine and radiator much further back in the chassis, and by using practically un-cambered springs, the whole appearance of the car has been altered. Yet the main components— engine, gears, axles and so on—are standard so far as internals are concerned. The engine has been rendered more efficient by considerable increase in engine ratio, by modifications to the timing gear, and by use of a bigger bore carburettor, but there is nothing unusual or freakish about it.

The body has slightly staggered seats, and the gear and brake controls are carried outside the body. The wings are the narrow-dome section type, leading straight to the short running boards. The space behind the seats is entered by pulling forward the seat squab.

A one-pane non-adjustable windscreen is fitted, and a sports-type hood is also included. The equipment comprises the usual dynamo-coil ignition and lighting system, electric horn, Smith 80mph speedometer, and Broadbent shock-absorbers.

The price is £145.

The Motor 27 September 1927: Two New Jowett Models

A Sports Car and an Attractive Coupé Added to the Range

The popularity of Jowett cars in Yorkshire cannot be doubted, as witnessed by the numbers encountered on the roads around Bradford and Leeds. The cars are actually manufactured in Idle, near Bradford, and they seem particularly suited to the undulating country in that neighbourhood.

The external appearance of the new sports Jowett is entirely different to any model that has preceeded it, but the components used in the make-up of the chassis are practically identical to those used in the standard production. The power unit is mounted some 9 inches to the rear of the usual position, while the radiator is placed rearwards a like amount. The alteration to the layout not only assists in providing a sporting appearance, but also helps materially to cut down vibration when travelling at speed by shortening the propshaft. The wheelbase and track dimensions remain the same as on the short wheelbase model touring car, but lighter springs fitted with shock absorbers, have been found necessary to compensate for the general reduction of weight of the sporting body compared with ordinary touring types.

The two-cylinder horizontally opposed engine with a bore and stroke of 75.4mm and 101.5mm respectively (capacity 907cc) has not been altered in dimensions or layout, but a higher compression ratio has been obtained by fitting different pistons. The standard gearbox and ratios are employed, which gives the car a very desirable liveliness, while, by virtue of the increased revs of which the engine is capable, a maximum speed approaching a mile a minute can be obtained.

The body accommodates a 6-foot driver and passenger without them being cramped in any way, and the seats are staggered some 4-inches in order to keep the body as narrow as possible. A very long bonnet serves another useful purpose besides enhancing accessibility of the power unit generally, in that it provides plenty of leg room.

Behind the seats a locker is situated with a capacity for at least two petrol cans, or of course, the equivalent amount of luggage. Access to this compartment is obtained by removing the seat squab of the driver's and passenger's seats. Long sloping front wings are supported on a substantial tubular framing, the latter also providing the means for mounting the headlamps, which incidentally, are the double filament type, thereby dispensing with side lamps.

We had an opportunity of taking both cars for a short road test in the hilly districts of Yorkshire. Right from the start it was apparent that the new sports model possesses powers of acceleration and hill-climbing markedly in advance of any previous standard Jowett model. This must largely be attributed to the fact that the engine of the sports model has been 'hotted up' somewhat and the weight of the complete vehicle is considerably reduced. Actually, the sports model empty weighs only 8cwt & 1 quarter, so that even with two heavy passengers the total weight would only be slightly over half a ton. So as far as acceleration goes, the following times show that the engine is really capable of putting up quite a 'nippy' performance. From 10mph to 20mph required 6½ seconds, 10mph to 30mph 13 seconds, while 20½ seconds were required to reach 40mph all on top gear. From a standing start 40mph could be attained in 15 seconds by making full use of the indirect gears.

Only fourteen of these were produced in 1928 before it was discontinued. Strictly speaking, this was a production model as opposed to a prototype, but as there were so few built, it seems appropriate to mention it here. Ironically, there appear to be several 'Sports-replicas' around today as many have been built over the last few years, including an actual Sports replica, Brooklands replica, Victoria Worsley replica, Sand racer, a 1929 trials car known as 'Polly', plus several others. Before long, we will have more replicas than the total production run of cars. The only original car to survive is the oldest, the 1923 example of Mike Koch-Osborne, described above.

This 1923 trials car was commissioned from the Jowett brothers by Major J. D. Johnstone, a famous trials driver at the time. It was a special lightweight car, which was used extensively during the 1920s and was the forerunner of the Jowett Sports that followed in 1928. (*LAT Photographic*)

The same car seen at the Jowett Car Club rally in Bideford in May 2009.

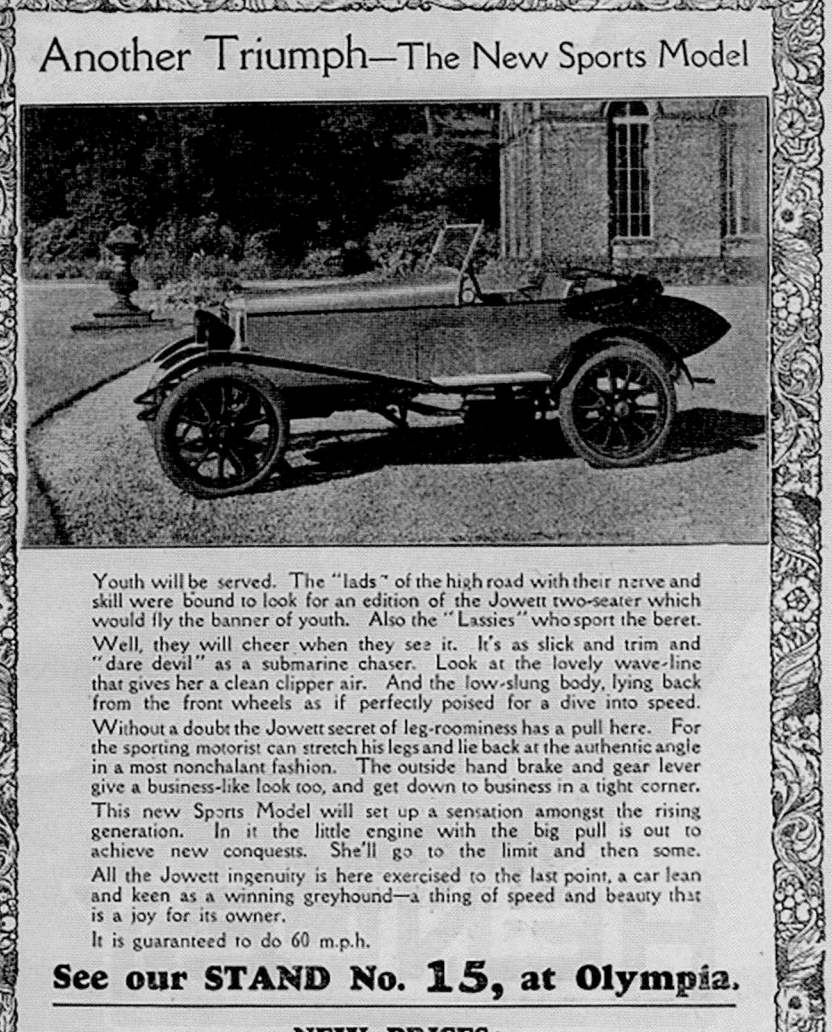

A wonderful full-page advert from *The Motor* dated 11 October 1927 advertising the Jowett Sport model, which was to be displayed on their stand at the Olympia Motor Show. (*The Motor*)

Another view of the 1928 Sport model taken from a 1928 sales brochure.

A period shot of a Jowett Sports model.

4

1930
JOWETT ARROW

THIS COMPANY WAS founded by an Arthur P. Compton in the autumn of 1929. Arthur Compton had already had a long career in coachbuilding at this time (including a spell at Jarvis of Wimbledon as both a designer and manager), having been associated with other similar businesses previously, some even bearing his name. Compton's company was established in south-west London in the borough of Merton where they began bodying Austin Seven chassis and naming the finished vehicles as the Austin Seven Arrow, of which a number still survive.

When the company moved to Hanwell in west London in the spring of 1930, he renamed his new premises 'Arrow Coachworks' and began fitting his recently designed two-seater open body to a series of rolling chassis, including the Morris Minor, Jowett 7, and Standard Little Nine. During the course of the next two years, the range of body styles increased dramatically with eight Minor variants being listed, varying in price from the Arrow Dart at £140 to the Arrow Sports Coupe at £196 10s 0d. Of the six body types fitted to the Minor chassis, four were fabric covered and two were metal panelled, these being the Spear open two-seater, based on an MG Midget, at £165 10s 0d, and the Foursome, a four-seater open touring car listed at £155. A feature of all the fabric covered models on offer was the option of a two-tone colour scheme at an additional cost of £6 10s 0d.

The extensive sales brochure for the Arrow range of models stated that their bodies could be fitted to the Standard 9, Wolseley Hornet, Singer 10, Singer Junior, Triumph, Morris Minor, Austin 7, and the Jowett 7, which was built on the long wheelbase chassis. There is a page dedicated to the Jowett in which it states that the wings were painted in Special Arrow Black; the wheels were black, and the exterior was also black with contrasting beads.

There must have been more of a choice of exterior colour than this as the Autocar Olympia Show edition describes a picture of the Jowett Arrow as: 'A smart and unusual Arrow sports body on a Jowett. The body extends partially over the mudguards and no running boards are fitted.' In its stand reports, the magazine said of A. P. Compton:

On a long wheelbase Jowett chassis is shown an example of the well-known two-seater Arrow body. which is fabric covered in blue and relieved by a white beading (the metal bonnet is a different colour from the fabric body). The upholstery is in red, and the little car is distinctly pleasing in appearance.

The sales brochure also goes on to say:

> The reputation of the Jowett is too well known to emphasized here, and in response to a large number of Jowett enthusiasts, we have produced the two-seater Jowett Arrow. You will note the very low body and riding position of this body, which will accommodate three persons abreast in moderate comport or two adults and a child in complete comfort and all under the hood. In bad weather, think of the advantage of this over the dickey seat, and how much more sociable, and still plenty of room for luggage picnic hampers etc etc, and all inside behind a squab that can be locked up.
>
> For Mr. Everyman this is undoubtedly the most reliable and economical car in its class.

The excellent *The Complete Jowett History* by Paul Clark and Ed Nankivell states that the total vehicle production of Jowetts in 1930 amounted to 2,603, of which four were long-rolling chassis. So that would confirm that the maximum number of Jowett Arrows in 1930 would have been limited to four. I would imagine that this will have been a real disappointment to Arrow, as it certainly looked like it was a very attractive little car. Sadly, no examples have survived.

In my opinion, this would be an ideal candidate for a replica to be built on a period chassis as it looked to be a lovely little car.

Close-up view of the Jowett Arrow. Sadly, no examples are known to have survived.

£165

COMPLETE

Also Mounted
on the following
Chassis

STANDARD 9
WOLSELEY
HORNET
SINGER 10
SINGER JNR.
TRIUMPH
MORRIS
MINOR
AUSTIN 7

FOR PRICES
SEE PAGE 16

ARROW 2 Seater
on Jowett Chassis

SPECIFICATION

WINGS — Arrow Special Black
WHEELS — Black
EXTERIOR — Black fabric
Contrasting Beads
INTERIOR COLOURS — Red, Green, Blue

Two Colour Scheme—Body, Wings
and Wheels £6 10 0 extra, net.

The Jowett Arrow

The reputation of the Jowett is too well known to be emphasised here, and in response to a large number of Jowett enthusiasts, we have produced the two-seater Jowett Arrow. You will note the very low body and riding position of this body, which will accommodate 3 persons abreast in moderate comfort, or two persons and a child in complete comfort and all under the hood. In bad weather, think of the advantage of this over the dickey seat and how much more sociable, and still ample room for luggage, picnic hampers, etc., etc., and all inside behind squab which can be locked up.

For Mr. Everyman this is undoubtedly the most reliable and economical car in its class.

A page from the very extensive Arrow sales brochure advertising the Jowett variant.

5

1933
La Roche

THE LA ROCHE prototype came into being in 1933–34 when Ben Jowett decided it was time to introduce a new power unit, as he was concerned at the limitations the flat twin 'little engine with the big pull' was becoming outdated. As far as Yorkshire folk were concerned, this would have been greeted with shock and horror, as under its bonnet was a vertical four-cylinder engine, with inlet-over-exhaust valve design, plus a Wilson pre-selector gearbox. The odd-looking saloon, bearing the badge La Roche on its unfamiliar radiator, with no mention of Jowett, was occasionally spotted travelling around the hills of Idle under the cover of darkness—the company did not want the public to think it was planning to discontinue the flat-twin. Two vehicles were completed before the project was abandoned in 1934.

The name 'La Roche' is said to be an anagram of 'chorale', which is a slow and stately song of praise, typically with a four-part setting, when it is known as chorale harmonisation. I like this anagram of chorale, as it is the most likely explanation to me, after reading so many of the Jowett 'flowery' adverts of the time, many of which have a musical theme.

The definitive description of this vehicle is in the excellent book *Jowett—The Complete History* by Paul Clarke and Ed Nankivell, which reads:

By 1933 it became evident that the 7hp engine did have its limitations in power and top gear flexibility, prompting Benjamin and his experimental teams to design a completely different power unit, loosely based on the Lanchester and Riley of the time. The four-cylinder vertical inline engine of 1½ litre capacity and 13½ hp RAC rating had pushrod operated overhead inlet and side exhaust valves, force fed lubrication, pump circulated coolant.

To take the weight of the heavier engine, Stephen Poole designed a cruciform-braced chassis (later adapted for the 1935 models) fitted with an enlarged version of the four-light Kestrel body with a foreshortened scuttle to allow for the larger engine. The radiator grille was altered to incorporate the word 'La Roche' which was an anagram of Choral—a slow dignified hymn.

Although a minimum quantity of 100 engine castings had to be purchased, just two prototype vehicles were constructed. One had a single Zenith down-draught carburettor with a ram pipe but no air cleaner, and a standard Jowett four-speed gearbox with a single dry plate clutch unit with the engine. The other had twin carburettors, and a Wilson pre-selector gearbox located midway down the prop-shaft, in conjunction with a fluid flywheel. This at first gave trouble with the adjusting bands.

The cars had sluggish low-speed pick-up due to the engine's exceedingly long stroke, which was little better than the Seven, but at higher speeds it was so brisk that the brakes had to be substantially enlarged to cope with the extra load.

Testing was mostly done under the cover of darkness to hide the fact that Jowett might be discontinuing its horizontally opposed two-cylinder engine. As development progressed, however, it became clear that to fully prove the design it was going to be a lengthy and expensive process. Furthermore, if a new car of suitable specification and durability was designed, it was felt that the cost of re-tooling the works could be prohibitive in view of the probable small output. It would not have been possible to combine the assembly of both types of engine, and therefore to adopt the new engine would entail the desertion of a proven market.

After the 'La Roche' project had been terminated in 1934—much to the annoyance of Benjamin, it was decided to pursue the quest for more speed by developing an engine that could be associated with their tradition of horizontal engines and that could be manufactured without major modification to their plant and machinery.

Over the years, I had numerous letters published in as many magazines and newspapers as I can think of, asking for Jowett information, which have resulted in me receiving hundreds of letters from ex-Jowett owners. Many of these have been published in some of my previous books on the Jowett marque and the club's magazine *The Jowetteer*. The letter that follows is one of the best I received as it related to a La Roche. As mentioned above, there were only two prototypes built, but somehow one of these was sold into private hands:

Recollections of a Curious Jowett: The 'La Roche' of 1933

I learned to drive during the war years on a 1933 30cwt Bedford van. The 'La Roche' car of which I write would doubtless be laid up in a garage somewhere at this time, due to wartime petrol restrictions. Thus, when the car was thrust upon me, in exchange for my 5cwt Singer van in 1950, it had probably been in use for some 12 years.

While looking distinctly old fashioned, it was one among many and quite 'Jowett-like' in many respects. Sturdy, it did not sink 'hammock' like in the middle as did most 1930's Jowetts beefed up a bit structurally, probably to carry the heavier engine and transmission. the gentle and somewhat furtive demo around the dark wet streets of Bradford's West Bowling was probably not the best preparation for ownership of this odd vehicle. Gentle for a reason apparent with the fullness of time, 'furtive' because of the blank space where the tax disc should have been!

A deal was done, the swap was made, and the 'fullness of time' was at hand. A top gear would have been useful, certainly of more use than the neutral that sat smugly in its place. Whilst today I would be glad to have this car alongside my 518i, I viewed it then, as my sole transport, a disaster. I would learn in the coming months more about 'it' than any car I have owned since. I was able to use the car in 'three speed mode' indeed, a journey to London and back was completed through a torrent of rusty rain in both directions. The radiator surround was sawing off the brass filler neck, I nearly lost the rad cap and the very handsome Calorimeter atop it.

A garage in Laisterdyke supplied petrol for the tank and air for the tyres. They sold Jowetts and knew the La Roche. 'Don't come for any parts for it, there aint any'! 'Then as an afterthought except for the diff case, that's the same as the 10hp, the ordinary 10'. Before I left, he suggested I have a chat with a Mr. Horace Grimley, 'he's the development engineer who knows all about it.'

I arrived in third gear at Mr. Grimley's lovely home at Harden, where he expressed his sympathy, 'that car' he said, 'was never intended to fall into the hands of the public!' He went on, 'Mr. Ben Jowett used the car for a long time, I myself used a sister car built at the same time. The sister differed in that your car has a fluid flywheel, mine had a Siddley type centrifugal clutch.

'This other car was broken up "early on" (whenever that was) and I intended that this car should be broken up as soon as the experiment was complete. I was begged by a colleague at Jowetts to let him have the car when I was finished with it. Against my better judgement I let him, and it moved around quite a bit since.' Mr. Grimley confirmed that the diff case was probably the only bit of the car that was standard with the production 10's of the time. 'There may be a few bits from the sister car which the colleague acquired.'

So, off to Bolton Villas, near the Jowett works, where I picked up cheaply, the road springs and two solid copper head gaskets, one of which I would later use. Whilst I had enthusiasm for the car, I had no practical skills. Thus, when I peeped inside the ENV/Wilson preselector gearbox the missing top gear was not revealed—a cone clutch taking the drive direct to the back axle. No way was I going to take it apart or re-assemble it myself.

However, I could remove the unit with little difficulty, and it was dispatched to a London firm which stated in the Autocar, 'Your Wilson &c gearbox reconditioned and returned in 48 hours'. They were as good as their word. At £45.17.6d I had spent 6 weeks wages in one go on a car that was worth about £35. My family paid the bill and I set about putting the car back together.

When it was finished and I sat on the empty crate, I failed to see the memo included with the packing, which referred to the 'smart response' (people didn't say slick in those days) I could expect from the new unit, as one might find the feel of a new clutch.

Those only familiar with the 'all singing all dancing' Borg Warner transmissions of recent years, should note here that this car had three pedals. The extreme left one triggered the shift which had been pre-selected at the steering column. The previous owner had not taken guidance in operating the gears and had used the third pedal as a clutch and this had led to a mellowing of the take up in the drive. The smart response was fine until the day came when a gear was missed, no big deal in a conventional set up, this wasn't conventional at all. What had all the inevitability of the Titanic v. the iceberg match. Revs soared, Daimler patent fluid flywheel taking on the solid mode, and ENV/Wilson box scrabbling for a gear before the revs went down, something had to give.

There would be a few more diff cases available for 10's today if it wasn't for me. I could buy them cheaply, two at a time. Being a little more careful in selection solved further breakages. Precision in the pre-selection of gears is more difficult to pass on to someone though. the 'someone' in the event was a young lady I had long worshipped, she a secretary, me much lower in the pecking order at the same company. But I had a car, I could drive, she didn't and couldn't.

She became a very good driver, I'm sure I helped in some way, but when the crown wheel and pinion went out through another diff case, she sought pastures new. Axles will fix, and by then I was quite proficient. Broken hearts take longer but seemingly are self-repairing. On that occasion the torque tube was lashed to the diff with rope, I think there was probably more mash than mesh in the fractured housing. The groaning growl as I drove home alone wasn't all from me.

I used to tell people I had a 'La Roche', 'looks like an old Jowett' they would say. I'd tell others I had an old Jowett, they disagreed, 'no Jowett has its engine standing up like that'. The 'standing up' IOE engine—probably a Meadows, was by now a cause of concern, nil oil pressure and a new noise deep down. When a big end bearing went, I was nursing the poor old car home to Bradford from Pontefract.

It is a tribute to the early design of such engines that someone of only average skill, using simple tools could lower the sump at the roadside and extract rod and piston from below and limp home, before darkness fell on three cylinders. A Jubilee clip giving a little more oil pressure than the missing big end bearing. I took a tram to Hindle Auto Engineers in Caledonia Street with an alloy con rod in my hand. 'Remetalling?—don't do much of that these days, it is 1952 you know! What size do you want it?' I hesitated, what did the crankshaft journal measure? I floundered, 'inch and a half, perhaps.' A man in overalls who worked to finer limits than 'inch and a half' came out and measured the journal. 'We can make it, but it won't last long, oval you know'. A kindly man, I noted his advice, 'When you get the rod back, put it all back together and get rid'. Neither he nor I could have guessed that here was what could have become a very unusual classic car, in fact the only one in the world. It went to the second-hand car trade for very little, old cars were plentiful, the Daimler Knight, a 1926 15hp that succeeded the La Roche cost me £30, two-thirds of the cost of the repairs to the ENY gearbox.

The 'La Roche' is history now, I'm glad I was part of it.

Ken Warnes, March 1991

The 1933 experimental four-cylinder in-line engine known as the La Roche. Only two were built and it did not reach production as the performance was disappointing. (*JCC Archive*)

A sketch of the bonnet badge for the La Roche by Ken Warnes, who owned the car. Normally, prototype cars were scrapped by the factory, but this one managed to find its way into private hands. Sadly, it was later scrapped.

6

1934
JOWETT EAGLE

THIS SUPERB CAR is owned by our club president, Malcolm Oliver. It has been on display at many Jowett Car Club rallies and other events and always creates a great deal of interest. The following article about this exact car appeared in the *Light Car* magazine on 20 April 1934 gave details as follows:

A Jowett Special Tourer—Godfreys Ltd, Introduce Attractive Body on Modified Chassis

A large number of motorists today want something a little out of the ordinary run of standard cars, both in the matter of appearance and performance. They do not necessarily want an out-and-out sports and a performance car, but they do appreciate the attractive lines of a sports tourer body and a performance just a little above that provided by a normal standard model.

To meet the needs for these people, special bodies mounted on standard or almost standard chassis are available for a large number of makes of car, but, in the main, the attractions of these models have been reserved for a chap who can pay upwards of £200.

Appreciating the fact there is an excellent opening in the under £200 class for cars of this type, Godfreys Ltd of 306 Euston Road, London NW1 have turned their attention to the Jowett chassis, which is, of course, well known for its reliability, economy and long life. The results of their efforts are to be seen in the very attractive Jowett Special Tourer shown in the illustrations on this page.

The price will be very moderate (about £170), but, in spite of this, the body is a really high-class job, whilst the chassis has been modified in certain minor respects to give a slightly better performance than standard without, however, in any way sacrificing smooth running or reliability.

To deal with the chassis alterations first, the engine has been fitted with special aluminium cylinder heads, which enable a slightly higher compression ratio to be used without loss of sweetness; an entirely new exhaust system has been adopted in which a separate pipe and silencer is used for each cylinder. The steering column has been raked to give a better driving position and a slightly higher back axle ratio is fitted (5½ to 1 in place of 5 3/8 to 1) to give effortless cruising and a good third gear performance. A different type of shock absorbers to improve road holding at speed are used. In addition, the radiator has been lowered slightly.

Turning now to the coachwork, one finds a really well-built body constructed on an ash framework with aluminium panelling and upholstery carried out in real leather. Full advantage has been taken of the size of the Jowett chassis and really roomy rear seats in which the occupants sit in, rather than on the car, are a feature.

An idea of the size of the rear seats is given in the fact that the overall width at the back is 39 inches with 35 inches between the arm rests, whilst the rear cushion measures 17 inches from front to back. The distance between its front edge and the back of the front seats is 18 inches with the front seat in its farthest forward position and 10 inches with the front seat placed right back – a position which none but the very tallest of drivers would find necessary.

This, however, is not the whole story, as there are deep footwells, the distance from the top to the rear cushion to the foot level in the rear being 19 inches. It will be seen from these figures that the Jowett Special Tourer is a full four-seater in every sense of the word and provides ample room for four people to tour in comfort. There is, incidentally, a large amount of luggage space in the tail.

So far as equipment goes, the car is well fitted out; standard features include front bumpers, an attractive facia-board panel embodying a 5-inch combined speedometer, single panel screen arranged either to fold flat, or to hinge from the top, as desired, a tandem screen wiper, pneumatic upholstery, sliding front seats, a spring-spoke steering wheel and twin-tuned electric horns.

Taken in all then, it will be seen that the Jowett Special Tourer is a really attractive car and a run on the road confirmed these impressions. Actually, the model tried did not embody the full chassis modifications, but, even so, the performance was livelier than that of the standard job. Timed over the quarter mile it reached a speed of 54.9mph, in one direction, whilst its mean speed was 50.3mph. These speeds accomplished on a very windy day which was not entirely favourable to getting the best out of the car. The standing quarter mile was covered in 20.6 seconds.

So far as the coachwork is concerned, the car proved very roomy and the general arrangement of the seats and controls distinctly good. Altogether, our impressions were that the car will meet with a very ready demand amongst those who want 'that little extra something' at an economical price both as regards initial cost and maintenance.

The car is being handled in the southern counties by Godfreys Ltd, in the Midlands by Hyde's of Birmingham, and in the north by Saxon Jefferies Ltd of Manchester.

I asked Malcolm if he knew how many Eagles had been built, and also where the name came from, as the above article just referred to it as being a Jowett Special Tourer; he replied:

Dear Noel, I have that article and there is also an almost verbatim article in *The Motor* dated April 1934.

I am of the understanding that this was the only one, however Michael Sedgwick suggested in 1963 when accepting a 'for sale' advert for the car, that it might have been 'one of the prototypes of the production Weasel'. Then Another advert appeared in *Veteran & Vintage* magazine July 1965— Jowett 'Weasel' Prototype (1934) 76,000 miles. V.G.C. £65 o.n.o. The car was also advertised prior to that in SJCC newsletter of June 1963, again as a Weasel prototype.

With regard to the name, I assume this is as a result of it being built by E. J. Newns as 'Eagle Coachworks' was their trademark. There was also a British Salmson 'Eagle' and a Lagonda Rapier 'Eagle'.

Best wishes, Malcolm 4/01/2018.

Above and below: The 1934 'Jowett Eagle'. This is the actual car that was described in an article in the 20 April 1934 issue of *The Light Car*, described as a 'Jowett Special Tourer—Godfreys Ltd, introduce an attractive body on a modified chassis.' These pictures were taken at the Jowett Car Club national rally in May 2015 in Macclesfield.

Above and below: Two more views of the 1923 Sports and the 1934 Eagle with a 1932 Blackbird Saloon taken at the Jowett Car Club rally at Tewksbury in 2016.

7

1939
Jowett 10-hp Sport

AN INTERESTING ARTICLE appeared in our club magazine, *The Jowetteer*, in February 1983, written by a gentleman called Charles J. Mitchell. It related to a 'one-off Jowett 10-hp Special', which had strong connections to the Jowett factory and Willie Jowett himself. Charles went on to say:

I am writing to you because of a family connection with Jowett Cars Ltd. My father's brother was Harry Mitchell, who was Managing Director of Jowett Cars between about 1926 to 1928. My father was a builder, and his Company rebuilt the works after the fire.

The fire Charles refers to here took place on 3 September 1930 when a huge fire swept through the factory which gutted most of the complex. It was thought that a workman had left a gluepot switched on at the end of his shift which caught fire during the night. Charles went on to say:

I enclose photographs of this one-off open sports four-cylinder Jowett that I helped to build. It belonged to Joe Haigh, who was the son of Gladney Haigh who was the buyer for Jowett Cars Ltd, and the design was approved by Willie Jowett. It was built on a standard wood saloon body base, and we had some assistance from the works in building the scuttle and making the hood. Sark made the radiator [I assume they were local car radiator producers], which was three inches lower than the standard saloon, it was also chromium-plated on the shell.

Joe Haigh, who I have lost touch with, is sitting in the back seat, my cousin, Rowland Lindley, who was killed on active service, who helped build the car, is sitting in the driving seat. The passenger was one of the many girls attracted by three smart lads and a one-off special sports car.

We called it 'Band Wagon' after the radio programme called 'Band Wagon'. The engine had a higher compression and stronger valve springs and the car weighed 14½ cwts. I remember going down the A1 from Bradford to Donnington and doing 30 miles in 30 minutes. We also took on a Riley 9 March Special and beat it! I was the practical man in building the body using as many standard parts as possible. The doors (which were cut down) were from the rear of the saloon, fixed at a steeper slope, hence the turned-up tails of the rear mudguards. I do not know where the car is now, it may well have been scrapped.

Sadly, there are no club records relating to CKW857 or the saloon registered CKY587, which appear in these photographs, so I must assume both cars were scrapped many years ago.

As there was such strong assistance from the factory, I feel it is appropriate to feature the car in this book, as it comes very close to being a potential prototype and looked a well-proportioned and attractive car. I feel sure that if a similar car had gone into production at this time, it would have been very popular. With the 10-hp four-cylinder engine fitted, I would have assumed it would have been quite lively. Jowetts only produced the 8-hp and 10-hp saloons during this period leading up to the Second World War.

Above, below, and next page: Four rather grainy views of the 1939 10-hp Sports Special registered CKW857 with a standard 10-hp saloon registered CKY587 built by Charles Mitchell and Joe Haigh with guidance from William Jowett. This was a one-off as Jowetts did not build a sporting 10-hp model, which is a shame as this looked like a super little car.

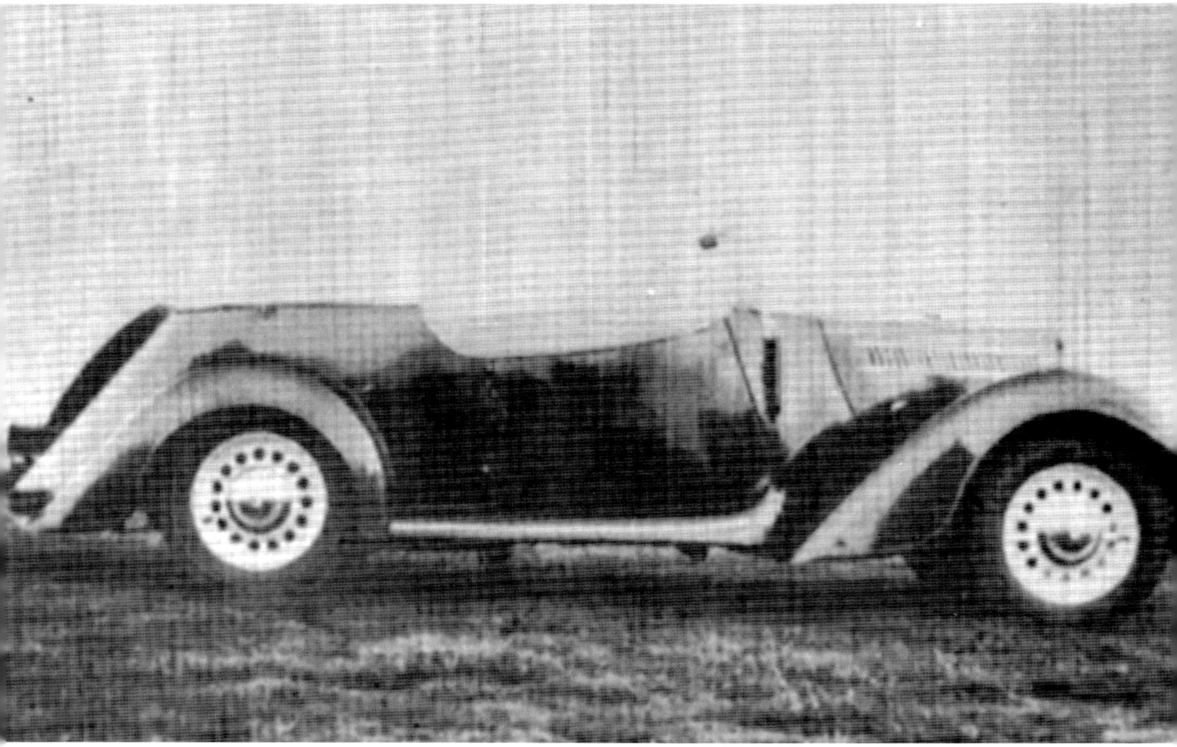

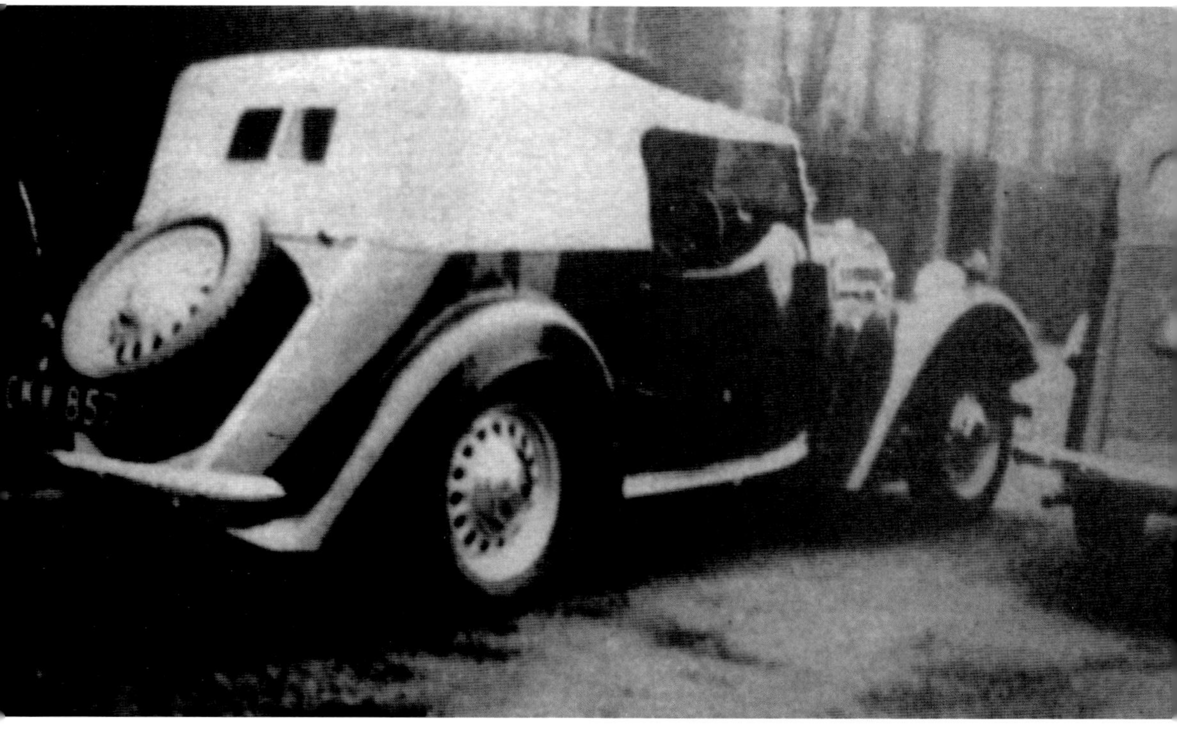

8

1942
Jowett Tractor

THIS IS AN interesting piece of Jowett history that is something of a mystery. This tractor is owned by Tom Blackwood in Scotland. The display noticeboard that he displays at the side of the tractor at rallies reads as follows:

This is a prototype and thought to be the only one made by Jowett Cars Ltd and was manufactured in the early part of World War 2.

The engine is a derivative of the famous 7hp flat twin boosted to 1050cc. It has four forward gears and a reverse. The transmission is solid worm drive and then roller train to the wheels (making it almost impossible to move unless under own power). A clutch is used to disengage inner wheel for sharp turns. The brake is on the transmission shaft and the implements lift is also operated by clutch from the transmission.

Due to Jowett's involvement with War armament work production was halted, but unlike vehicle production, did not get resurrected after the war.

It is probably just as well, Harry Ferguson had produced the 'Little Grey Fergie' and it is difficult to see how the Jowett could have competed with such advanced machinery, 'The Ferguson System'.

The tractor was featured in an article by Jim Bradley in the December 2007 issue of *Tractor & Machinery* magazine, referring to the tractor as a pre-production prototype built at the Jowett factory during the early part of the war:

The years between the wars were difficult for all but the largest companies and the small fry had to try really hard to stay in business. The Jowett Car Company, of Bradford in Yorkshire, was one such company. It had a fine record for making sturdy motor cars that were a tad pricey but lasted for ever in the way one associates with anything made in Yorkshire or, for those of a certain geography, 'up north'. To extend its range Jowett also made a wee van called a Bradford [*sic*.] [the pre-war Jowett light commercial was known as an 8hp van, the name 'Bradford' was used in 1946 on the post-war van, which was basically a re-vamped version of the pre-war model] featuring its flat-twin engine, that proved to be a very adaptable piece of kit and encouraged the company to experiment with diverse products such as generators and then a tractor for light cultivation.

HALTED BY WAR

Typically, Jowett went about developing with engineering skill and a determination that it would be soundly built and worth its price. It eventually produced a prototype tractor that was about to go into production when Herr Hitler and friends decided to hold a war. The tractor project was shelved as the output of the Jowett factory was turned over to war work. After hostilities ended the project failed due to shortage of materials and eventually Jowett was left with the Javelin car and its sporty cousin the Jupiter (and Bradford commercial vehicles!) to see out the end of this excellent company, that really deserved a better run of luck. By coincidence, the Jowett factory was used for many years after the company closed for the assembly of International tractors. Wandering around the 2007 Farming Yesteryear Rally at Scone Palace, I chanced upon a small tractor among the stationary engines, rather than the huge classes in the adjoining enclosures. It appeared different to anything I had seen before and an information board told something of what it was, a Jowett, the remaining information being supplied by the owner Tom Blackwood. In construction there are a few features that are almost unique to the Jowett, but first the basics.

The flat-twin 1050cc engine was a robust and nearly unburstable unit, delivering power where it worked best for the operator. A four-speed and reverse gearbox fed the worm-drive reduction box to chain drives for each rear wheel. This, in effect, meant there was no differential action for the driving wheels and for tight cornering. A pair of hand clutches was used to disengage the drive to the inner wheel of the turn, which meant that in use this was a tractor well suited to a driver blessed with three arms and hands. For normally limbed folk this took a little more dexterity but, with practice, it worked quite well.

ENGINEERING DETAIL

A transmission brake was the only means of slowing and stopping the tractor, other than by implement drag or driving into something hard. A drive taken from the transmission-powered implement lift gave rise to the thought that it might only function while the tractor was in motion, but the canny Jowett engineers probably got round that one in their usual way. Not too much is known of whatever working life the Jowett had, if any. It was found in reduced circumstances at Bookham, Surrey, by Don Yidbury, of Bramley, who is believed to have restored it before passing it on to Peter Ball, of Hedenbridge, thence to Tom Blackwood, a retired plant hirer, who has now owned it for three years at Stewarton, Ayrshire.

WHAT MIGHT HAVE BEEN

It might be fair to describe the Jowett tractor as the one that could never have been. Had development not been curtailed by war, it might have gone on to successful production, but in an austere post-war situation the odds of success were limited.

With fierce competition from a whole range of well-established light tractors, such as the Allis-Chalmers B and BMB President, and more than a few newcomers, market penetration would have been difficult.

But all of these minor makers were eventually to be swept away by the grey tide of the ubiquitous Ferguson TE tractor system as it re-wrote the textbook of farming across the whole world.

I am intrigued by one minor detail of the Jowett story. I cannot get my head around the notion that any manufacturer would only produce one example of a prototype.

I have no reason to doubt any who claim the Jowett is a one-off, but maybe only by survival. One day we might see another, or maybe more than one Jowett light tractor emerging from obscurity—most likely with an interesting tale to tell.

It is my understanding also that the tractor was built during the early part of the war as an exercise for Jowett apprentices. Its engine number confirms it is a 1942 example. It is fitted with large commercial vehicle rear wheels. Unfortunately, no one seems to know for sure why it was built, as there are no factory records relating to it.

I feel that it seems appropriate to include the tractor in this book, as many people think it was a prototype which did not go into production after the war—either way, it is an interesting little tractor that was built at the Jowett factory.

Above and opposite page: Three views of the 1942 Jowett tractor. It is not clear if this was a prototype tractor that did not go into production or an apprentice's exercise. This was the only example built as far as I am aware.

Another view of the 1942 Jowett tractor, taken this time at the club's rally in Peebles in 2017.

9

1943
Gabo Javelin

IT HAS TO be said that I find this whole project rather strange, as all of this seemed to have been taking place at a similar time that Jowetts had headhunted Gerald Palmer from the Nuffield Group in 1942 with the brief to build the all-new Jowett model, which, of course, became the Javelin. Callcott Reilly, the managing director of Jowetts, allowed Gerald to work on the Javelin, but also other designs for the bodywork were considered.

One design in particular was considered by a Russian émigré called Naum Gabo, an abstract artist and sculptor who was working at the London-based Design Research Unit. This unit was set up in 1942 by Herbert Read and Marcus Brumwell. Read wrote to Gabo on 12 May 1943 saying that the Jowett board had agreed in principle to pay a sum of £3,000 spread over three years for the design and a further £3,000 if the designs were accepted. It is hardly surprising to me that the design was rejected by the board as being too futuristic and too expensive to produce. The design, in my opinion, has more of the feel of a continental design house and would have appealed more to, say, Citroen or Panhard?

Gerald's design of the Javelin bodywork was very futuristic at the time, and I am pleased to say that the Jowett board chose his design, which was a much more viable proposition, and of course, was a great success. More details of Design Research Unit appear in the quote listed below taken from the Tate Modern website:

Held within the Tate archive is a series of photographs, drawings and notes that relate to Naum Gabo's brief 1940s venture into car design. Conceived as a dramatically integrated form, the car appears more streamlined and aerodynamic than other British vehicles of that era, a curvilinear body with recessed door handles and headlights. Among the detail consistent with his sculpture from the period, Gabo employed a spiral motif in the grille and biomechanical forms such as a kidney-shaped steering wheel. His design incorporated a curved Perspex windscreen and nylon upholstery—two new plastics he had begun to use elsewhere in his work.

The project was one of the first originated by the Design Research Unit, a loose association of architects and industrial and graphic designers that grouped together during the Second World War to form a new practice with Gabo's friends, the critic Herbert Read and patron Marcus Brumwell. It sits at the beginning of the fascinating journey of an important but lesser-known initiative in the history of British design. The Design Research Unit was a socially minded operation whose roots lay in the first multi-disciplinary advertising firms of the 1920s and a chance grouping of individuals in the Ministry of Information. Its formation can be traced back to discussions in 1942 that produced some early notes proposing an advisory body of specialists serving government and trade alike that could be consulted on all aspects of design.

David Goodway in his book *Herbert Read Reassessed* also referred to the Naum Gabo concept design for the Javelin as follows:

It was in these years—the early 1940s—that Read was entering the practical world of design. This happened through the Design Research Unit (DRU). This was an idea for a design practice that could provide 'new designs' in the reconstruction that would come after the war. Each of the three words of the name of this outfit—design, research, unit—was loaded with the promise of something modern, rational, scientific.

Design Research Unit was formulated in 1942 by Marcus Brumwell and Herbert Read. Brumwell worked in advertising and was one of the enlightened left-leaning patrons in modernism in Britain then. One finds him now in the footnotes in British cultural history as a patron of artists – among them Ben Nicholson, Naum Gabo and Piet Mondrain.

DRU started operations in London in 1943. At the start, while other partners were involved in war work, Read was in sole charge of the DRU's office. A year or two later he became less centrally involved; attending directors' meetings, and perhaps also weekly meetings where current work was criticised. One of their early projects suggests that, at the outset, DRU was a rather literal attempt to implement the ideas of Art and Industry; the abstract artist finding a social role. This was the design of a car body, which the artist Naum Gabo carried out for Jowett Cars. There was some altruism here on the part of Brumwell and —it would have been a way to get some money to Gabo—but certainly the project came to nothing, beyond sketches and models.

As can be seen from the pictures of the clay model and scale model, the car was too futuristic to be a viable proposition in early post-war Britain. The project got no further than the scale model, so it was an expensive exercise for Jowetts. Thank goodness it was Gerald's Javelin design that the Jowett board accepted.

An artist's impression of the 1943 Naum Gabo proposed design of the Javelin. (*Tate Gallery*)

Scale model of the proposed Naum Gabo Javelin. (*Tate Gallery*)

Two views of the painted model of the Naum Javelin. Unsurprisingly, this design was not acceptable to the Jowett board, so the project was abandoned. This made way for the Gerald Palmer, design of the Javelin, which was far more impressive car. (*Tate Gallery*)

10

1948
JAVELIN WITH PERSPEX ROOF

A S FAR AS I am aware, there were two Javelins produced with a Perspex sunroof fitted. The first was chassis number D8/PA/188, which was registered to Jowett Cars Ltd on 23 June 1948. It was coloured golden sand with brown leather trim and registered FKU372. This car was used by Gerald Palmer, the car's designer, on a testing trip to Sweden in the summer of 1948. Sadly, this car has disappeared without trace, probably by the early 1960s.

The second was chassis number D8/PA/1001 and was the property of Charles Callcott-Reilly, who took over as managing director of Jowett Cars Ltd in early 1939. This car was registered for the road on 18 November 1948 with a Bradford registration number: FKW318. It was originally turquoise blue with beige trim. The Perspex sunroof was going to be advertised as an optional extra, but it was never put into production, which made these cars unique. The car was exhibited at the Geneva Motor Show in 1948; it was also displayed at the Earls Court Motor Show in London, later in the year. It shared the Jowett stand with a black Javelin and the one-off Javelin Convertible, which is described in a separate chapter.

Clearly, the car was not registered for the road until after the two motor shows in 1948 prior to Charles Callcott-Reilly taking delivery of it. Soon after this, he was forced off the board of the company. He left to form Cyclemaster, which produced small engines that fitted into cycles and mopeds.

Sometime after, Arthur Booth, who was the foreman of the Experimental Department at Jowetts, left and joined Cyclemaster as the head of the service department there. During 2012, I was in correspondence with Neil Hinchley, who was Arthur's son-in-law; he went on to tell me:

During the 1940s the comedian Norman Evans ('over the garden wall') always insisted that Arthur serviced his car. So pleased was he with Arthur's efforts that he always supplied tickets for a complimentary box at the annual pantomime at the Bradford Alhambra, for Arthur and his family to attend.

He also worked on prototype cars and frequently had to give them test runs. These trips provided rare trips to the seaside for the family. It was during this period that he purchased a prototype Javelin, the development costs of which were £30,000! Obviously, he didn't pay anything like that.

During the war he worked on munitions development—including hardening metals to resist enemy fire etc. When Jowetts opened a factory at Clayton, Arthur moved there, and the family moved to Hawton Grange Road. My wife is not sure why, but Arthur never really settled at this site (it could be that someone was promoted over him). He left Jowetts in December 1950 and moved to Kenton, Middlesex where he worked for Cyclemaster (small petrol engine mounted in the back wheel of a bicycle).

Harry Gill was employed at Jowetts from 1924 right through the war but left in 1954 when he was working in the service department. He also went to work for Cyclemaster, working for Arthur Booth again. He recalled his memories of the car in 1975:

I remember the Javelin with the perspex roof, it was finished in turquoise blue and trimmed in beige hide. My first acquaintance with it was during my time in the Experimental Department whilst working on the Bradford production. At that time Arthur Booth was the foreman of the department. I remember that on one occasion we took the car into Bradford and a crowd gathered round when we parked it in Bank Street in the centre of the city. I little realised that I would meet up with the car again some years later in London after having left Jowetts and joined Cyclemaster.

Some of Cyclemaster's directors were Palmer Phillips, Charles Callicot Reiley and a Scotsman called John McGregor. Arthur Booth was also with the company in the Service Department, near Battersea Bridge. It was here that I renewed my acquaintance with the car, which by then had become Arthur Booth's personal vehicle.

I joined the company as foreman of the Service Department and lived in lodgings at Clapham Common, a short distance away—my wife and family were still living in Bradford. During this time the company (and particularly Mr. Booth) were very kind to me. About every three or four weeks they either paid my return rail fare to Bradford or loaned me a vehicle—paying all the expenses—to enable me to spend the weekend with my family. I usually left Battersea (and later Byfleet) after work on the Friday and reached Bradford in the early hours of Saturday morning, returning Sunday afternoon (or about midnight in summer) to arrive back in time for work on Monday morning.

I used different types of vehicles including a Bradford van and utility, and once used a 5-ton Bedford truck so as to make a delivery of Cyclemaster units to Leeds. Also, I used the Javelin, and one trip in particular stands out in my mind.

It was winter and the country generally was snowbound. I left about the usual time and progress was good in the London area, but as I went further north the snow was much heavier and packed hard on the road by passage of snow ploughs. It was usual in the areas around towns to spread sand and soil to aid traffic. This caused the surface to break up into huge potholes. My progress was very slow. The cold seemed to strike down from the roof, even if the blind was in use. I found that without the blind in use the flicker of the streetlights reflecting on the dashboard and windscreen was troublesome. The car ran faultlessly on this and the return journey.

At a later date two cars (I think) were being sent to Australia and were driven to Tilbury Docks. When I was testing early Javelins, I found that when changing from first to second it occasionally happened that there was partial engagement of another gear. When this occurred it almost brought the car to a standstill. By juggling the gear lever while the engine was running, and the clutch disengaged it was possible to restore things to normal. At any rate one of the cars destined for Australia was immobilized in a shed on the wharf at Tilbury. Mr. T Hopkins, the Assembly Superintendent, decided to go and rectify the trouble with me as a member of the Service Department. We used one of the prototype cars with the V screen (EKW303) and loaded the boot with my tools, and one of the trolleys we used for engine removal, and a spare gearbox. We left during the afternoon and arrived in the early evening and were directed to the appropriate shed. The gear lever was jammed between first and second, I started the engine with the clutch disengaged, joggled the lever and the gears were once more back to normal. After testing the car around the shed, gear changing took place as it should.

At the time the gearboxes were made by Meadows, and I assumed that testing had been carried out before delivery to us. It was not realised, at any rate in the Production Department, that accurate adjustment of the selectors was required. A memo to this effect was later issued from the Experimental Department.

Our return journey to Bradford was not as pleasant as the outward one and I dimly remember being lost somewhere near London in a slight fog, and struggling to keep awake, at the same time feeling chilled to the bone!

In 2010, I was in correspondence with Jean Bexley in Attleborough, Norfolk, who was Harry's daughter. She still had her father's notebook, which detailed his time with Jowetts:

Dear Mr Stokoe, after reading the article 'The glory days of Jowett' which was published in the October 2009 issue of *The Dalesman* magazine, I am writing to tell you about my father.

Harry Esmond Gill began at the Jowett factory in Idle, Bradford in 1923 as a 14-year-old apprentice. He died many years ago but carried out many duties whilst working for the Company. The following notes have been taken from his notebook which is now in my possession.

His first twelve months were passed in the Engine Testing Department, followed by work in various parts of the Assembly Shop. In 1929 he transferred to Rectification, road testing, finishing and final inspection, he also spent some time in the Service Department. By 1939 the factory had switched to munitions work and he was in charge of a department housed in the Bradford Power Station. Here they dealt with the repair and assembly of Air Force ground equipment, including bomb trolleys.

After the war he assisted in the development of the Bradford van and the Javelin prototypes. Then, as foreman of finished cars, he went on the road to test Jupiters in chassis form, for 100 miles each.

At the end of car production in 1953, he worked in the Service Department, repairing crashed and damaged cars and servicing them. In 1954 he was offered a new job with Cyclemaster Ltd in Battersea, I understand that the Manager and some of the Directors were previously involved with Jowett Cars Ltd, and now worked for Cyclemaster.

It is interesting to see that Charles Callcott-Reilly, Arthur Booth, and Harry Gill all worked for Jowett Cars Ltd, and all ended up working at Cyclemaster. Clearly, Charles persuaded Arthur and Harry to join him in his new company. All three of them drove the Perspex-roofed Javelin FKW318 and the split-screen Javelin prototype EKW303.

Sadly, the Perspex-roofed Javelin FKW318 was almost beyond economic restoration when it was known to the club back in the mid-1980s, but sadly, it was owned by somebody who would not sell it as they were going to 'restore it one day'. He has since died, by which time the car was in its final stages of decrepitude. All the salvageable parts still on the car were removed in 2020, including the sunshine roof, which had a crack in it back in the 1980s, but has been taken as a template for anybody brave enough to fit one to another Javelin. It is such a shame that this unique car should receive such a sad demise; it deserved a better fate than this.

You're going to like . . .

its extra *roominess*

Remarkable, that a car of moderate size should be so roomy and comfortable. Four ride regally, with armrests between them. Lift armrests and there's room for six. The boot is big enough to take all luggage. And there's excellent visibility all round, including, as an optional extra, a transparent plastic half-roof. Price £640, plus purchase tax £178.10.7

The JOWETT **JAVELIN** new right through

The first Javelin with Perspex sunroof, seen here on a test drive to Sweden by Gerald Palmer, the designer of the Javelin. This car was first registered to Jowett Cars on 23 June 1948.

Opposite page: An early advert for the all-new Javelin. It clearly shows the Perspex sunshine roof, which was going to be an optional extra. This car was one of only two built to my knowledge and it was not proceeded with.

These two pictures were taken from a short Pathé film of the 1948 Swiss Motor Show, held in Geneva in March that year featuring one of the Perspex-roofed Javelins. The second picture shows the driver about to draw the fabric curtain over the Perspex roof. (*Pathé News*)

The second Javelin with a Perspex sunroof. It was first registered on 13 November 1948 to Charles Calcott-Reilly, the managing director of Jowett Cars Ltd. Arthur Booth, who was foreman of the Experimental Department at Jowetts, often brought Jowett cars he was testing home at lunch time and on trips to the seaside; his wife, Doris, is pictured with the car. Arthur did in fact go on to buy the split-screen Javelin prototype registered EKW303. (*A. Booth*)

The car was bought by G. Mitchell on 25 November 1966. It was pictured here in the 1980s, by which time the car was barely restorable.

Mr Mitchell died in 2019, by which time both this car and a Jupiter were beyond restoration. The few salvageable parts from the Javelin have now been removed.

11

1948
JAVELIN CONVERTIBLE

THE JAVELIN CONVERTIBLE, or drophead, was displayed on the Jowett stand at the 1948 Earls Court Motor Show. It was a surprise to the motoring press when they first saw it. I have always been fascinated by this car, and as you will see, I had been in correspondence with its owner, Dennis Cremer, since the 1980s. He told me that he bought the car in 1965 in a very derelict state, and he had worked on it right until his death in 2019.

It was when I was at the 1994 Jowett Car Club National Rally at Gloucester Docks that I was able to glean a little more information on the convertible Javelin. The guest of honour was Gerald Palmer (the designer of the Javelin). I had corresponded with him regularly before, but this was the first time that I had been able to have a good chat with him.

I asked him if he had been involved in the convertible Javelin project, which he gave an emphatic 'no' to. He said that the car had been built up by a specialist coachbuilder, which he thought was in London. He also said that he was in fact rather annoyed at it being on the show stand at Earls Court as he felt that it detracted from the two Javelins that were on the stand with it as there were still long waiting lists for the car and very few Javelins were on UK roads at that time. He went on to say that it was the first time he saw it when it was on the stand, and he did not think the proportions at the rear of the car were correct. Sadly, Gerald died in 1999; he was a charming unassuming man, I was so pleased to have met him on several occasions.

This is how the car was described in the motoring press at the time. As can be seen, the car was just as much of a surprise to them as it was to Gerald Palmer:

The Motor, 27 October 1948

> Javelin Drop-head Coupé—in response to demands from abroad, the Jowett Company has developed this drop-head coupé on the Javelin chassis which will be seen for the first time on the Jowett stand at Earls Court. Three persons can be accommodated on the front bench-type seat while a dicky-seat allows two additional passengers to be carried.

The Autocar, 29 October 1948: Jowett—Stand 174

Great changes since the war have come from this old-established Yorkshire firm, so well-known for its flat-twin economy car. The new car is the Javelin one of the most modern small cars in the world today and a design which British industry can be proud.

There are three models on the manufacturer's stand a four-door saloon in gold, the standard finish (£818 10s 3d including purchase tax) a turquoise-coloured saloon, which colour is a metallic finish, and a roadster type coupé, which is a show surprise. Except for the new body, there are no changes in specification.

All these three have a similar 8-foot 6-inch wheelbase in a chassis frame that is integral with the steel saloon and with a horizontally opposed four-cylinder engine of 1,486cc mounted ahead of the front wheels. Torsion bars are used for the suspension of all four wheels, the front being independently sprung. The various technical advantages of the Javelin are clearly stressed by the examination of a cut-away chassis and engine.

List Price, Saloon £640 plus British Purchase Tax £174 10s 7d

Drop-Head Coupé £750 plus British Purchase Tax £209 1s 8d

Garage & Motor Agent, October 1948

In response to urgent demands from overseas agents, the Jowett Company has developed a Javelin drop-head coupé which makes its appearance on the Jowett stand at Earls Court.

Designed as a 2 to 3-seater with ample luggage space and with a dicky to accommodate two occasional passengers, this model will find ready acceptance in Switzerland and Scandinavian countries, for which markets it has primarily been developed.

It will become available to the home market at £750 plus £209 1s 8d Purchase Tax.

Mechanically, this Javelin drop-head is identical to the saloon and, in fact, the steel pressings used in the saloon wings and bonnet are all employed but aluminium doors and aluminium panelled tail all help to keep the weight down, so there is a gain of approximately 1 cwt over the saloon version.

The standard bench-type front seat has been retained with centre folding armrests and armrests on the doors. At 51 inches wide, this seat accommodates three abreast, or gives an impressive amount of room when there are only the driver and one passenger. The curved screen and the floor clear of obstruction both feature on the Javelin saloon are also to be found on the drop-head coupé, but a more 'coachbuilt' appearance has been given to the styling by the employment of veneer walnut finishing rails on top of the facia and door trim. The facia panel itself is covered in leather cloth matching the leather upholstery.

Behind the driving compartment is a roomy luggage tonneau 5 feet wide by 2 feet deep. In this the flush fitting folding head disappears when the car is opened, and if extra passengers are carried in the dicky seat, ample foot-room is provided for them, but basically it is a roomy space for luggage.

Access to the dicky seat is facilitated by steps mounted on the rear wing, and behind the dicky is a separate compartment carrying the standard Javelin layout and providing additional storage space for coats, rugs and small luggage.

The folding head is in beige cloth, leather bound, and tones with the claret exterior finish the car, with its long-swept tail, combines dignity and rakishness in good balance.

The Motor, 3 November 1948: Jowett—Stand 174

New on the Jowett stand is an attractive drop-head coupé first illustrated in *The Motor* last week. As with the saloon (two examples of which were also exhibited), the wide body provides three-abreast accommodation but in this case, there is no rear seat, a large space under the hood is available for luggage. Aft of the hood is a dicky seat (room for which is provided by the space already mentioned) and behind the dicky is a conventional luggage locker of moderate size.

Also, of more than usual interest on the stand is a sectioned saloon cut away to show the advanced design of this noteworthy post-war model. Amongst its many features are a horizontally opposed OHV four-cylinder 1,486cc water-cooled engine developing 50bhp at 4,400rpm which, owing both to its compact layout and forward mounting, makes exceptional body space available within a modest wheelbase. Also of note is the suspension system, for which torsion bars are used all round, the front wheels being located by wishbones and the non-independent rear axle by pairs of trailing arms with the torsion bars, in this case, set across the frame.

STEP UP—The Jowett Javelin Coupé is one of the few exhibits with a dicky seat, this being reached by two steps on the offside of the body, as shown.

The car is also mentioned in David Culshaw's *Motor Guide to Makes and Models* published in 1959 and also in the recent book *Cars in the UK 1945–1970* by Graham Robson.

Details of the Car's History from the Logbook

Jowett Javelin Drop-head Coupe, 1486 cc, chassis number D8/PA/251, colour Indian red. First registered 27 May 1949.

First owner: Jowett Cars Ltd, Bradford Road, Idle, Bradford, registered 27 April 1949.

Second owner: Law Sons & Dean, Jowett Agents, Tweedale Street, Rochdale, registered 10 April 1952.

Third owner: Joan Wolstenholme, 84A Todmorden Road, Summit, Littlebrough, Lancashire, registered 21 July 1956.

Forth owner: Ronald Bartram, 9 Westgate, Whitworth, Rochdale, Lancashire, registered 14 January 1959.

Fifth owner: Dennis Fraser Cremer, 6 Hawthorne Terrace, Cockenzie, East Lothian, date of registration not shown, but was about 1965.

At Dennis's request, I wrote to the *Rochdale Observer* in my official capacity of press officer and librarian of the Jowett Car Club to see if they would publish a request for information on the car, as it was in the Rochdale area between 1952 and 1965. I also told them that this was a unique one-off prototype Jowett which had been rescued by Dennis. My request was much reduced, but it was published in the paper on Saturday, 8 February 1992, and read as follows:

Wanted—Full-Service History of a One-Off Car

Only one was ever built, and for ten years it travelled the roads of Rochdale.

It was a Jowett Javelin saloon convertible, a car which made its debut at the Motor Show in Earls Court in 1948. Now the Jowett Car Club is trying to trace its history.

It was rescued from near the Buckley Mills, Halifax Road in the mid-1960s, as many of the mills were being demolished. Its condition at the time was described as poor, but restoration work is being done by a club member in Scotland, who hopes to have it running next year.

The car was built as a prototype at the Jowett works in Bradford, Yorkshire [*sic*.] but never went into production.

After Earls Court, the car was owned by Rod Law, director of Law, Sons & Dean, Jowett's Rochdale agents.

During the 1950s it was registered to Joan Wolstenholme of Todmorden Road, Summit, Littlebrough and in 1959 to Ronald Bartram, Westgate, Whitworth.

The club is eager to contact the car's two registered owners, or anyone who may have known them.

Information, and if possible, photographs, would be greatly appreciated.

I was delighted as this request created a lot of interest and I had several interesting letters about the car, the first of which was from Mrs Joan Burrill (formerly Miss Joan Wolstenholme):

Dear Mr Stokoe, having read the *Rochdale Observer* dated 8th February 1992, I thought that this time I must really put pen to paper and tell you that I am Mrs Joan Burrill (formerly Miss Joan Wolstenholme) the first private registered owner of the Jowett Javelin convertible car registered FKY619.

I did actually see the cutting from the *Rochdale Observer* dated 12th March 1986, but at that time I did not fully realise that it was such a rare and prestigious car. Hence, I let that go without replying to Mr. Dennis Cremer of Midlothian; like you, he was wanting me to contact him with information about the car.

Firstly, let me tell you that this car was bought for me by my Mum, being a belated 21st birthday present, because when I was actually 21 cars were a little difficult to obtain as regards how long you had to wait for a specific colour. So, with my 21st birthday well and truly passed, it was I think 1956, when this car was bought for me. I was at the time looking for a Morris Minor and dithering about the colour and whether to have a saloon or a soft-top convertible when I went to the Jowett agents in Rochdale, Messrs. Law Sons & Dean the car being intended for Mr Law. This car stood out in the showroom, polished and admired by their staff. I was told that although the car was not exactly new by the year of manufacture, it was in pristine condition. The price was £500 which was more than the new Morris Minor or equivalent. I really wonder why Mr Law worried to sell it or should I say he allowed me to buy it.

Being of the female sex I have nothing to relate regarding the mechanical history of the car, nothing ever went wrong with it, and I can only describe these little anecdotes.

I was very proud to have this as my first car, maroon in colour with a cream steering wheel and tan leather seats, the front being a bench type. Obviously, I had to take my driving test, and as I had learned with the British School of Motoring, I took my first test in one of their cars and failed, so second time around I was determined to take it in my own car with the hood down, so I was hoping for a dry day, otherwise the examiner would not have been too keen on getting wet.

I have had the only two photos I have reproduced for you. I am the driver, my Mum and my office friend, Betty Goodwin, are in the back.

Before I passed my test it was sometimes not easy to get a driver to sit with me, and at this stage I can tell you it gave me the chance of meeting my future husband, but that is another story!

Joan Burrill, Littleborough, Lancashire, 25th February 1992.

Other replies I received to my request are listed below:

Dear Mr Stokoe, reference the article in the *Rochdale Observer* on 8th February.

I rescued the Jowett Javelin 2-seater convertible from a cottage in the hills above Whitworth in about 1965, it had been laying outside in moorland conditions for about two years, the owner at that time was Mr Bartram.

About the same time a photo appeared in *Motor Sport* of a one-off Jowett van owned by a George Mitchell from Kinross, a Jowett enthusiast (as I was). That same year I met him at the annual Jowett Car Club Weekend at Harrogate he told me about a chap in Edinburgh, who was trying to find my car. He arrived at my place the following week to have a look at it. He was the Secretary of the Scottish Section of the Jowett Car Club and called Dennis Cremer.

At that time, I lived in Buckley Mill Yard (mentioned in the article), I also had a small engineering shop in the mill yard, and when Dennis walked into my workshop, he could not believe his eyes. I had a 1922 Alvis (less its radiator) and he had a 1923 Alvis and a spare radiator. We had a long chat about Alvis and Jowetts and eventually we did a deal which included the Alvis radiator!

The next week he returned with a trailer and took the 2-seater to Edinburgh. At the time he worked at the University of Edinburgh Department of Zoology. We kept in touch until about 1974 or 1975, and the last I heard of the car was in 1985. I was told it was in a museum in the Border region of Scotland.

Mr Law of Law Sons & Dean (the first private owner) told me that the car had been made for the Paris Motor Show in 1948 and was originally a left-hand-drive car [*sic*.]. This was borne out by the toe hole just forward of the rear wing and step on top of the rear wing being on the off-side which would have been on the near-side of a right-hand-drive car. It was designed for the French market as it was so like the Citroen Light 15 two-seater of 1936-39, but more modern. It did not catch on so they switched it to right-hand-drive and displayed it at Earls Court in 1948.

I hope this is of interest to you, kind regards.

Phil Shepherd, Rochdale, Lancashire, February 1992.

From the late 1980s, I was in regular correspondence with Dennis about the convertible Javelin until his death in 2019. These are some excerpts of some the letters during this time:

Dear Noel,

I heard of the car from George Mitchell and eventually persuaded him to tell me where it was. At that time, I was the Registrar of the Jowett Car Club. I went down to Rochdale to fetch it from a Phil Shepherd. He had rescued it from a field where it had spent some time. It was in very poor condition, and I still do not know how it did not break in half on the way home!

It was shifted from garage to garage and through the hands of 'car restorers' until recently, when I started work on it again. It is a real struggle with two steps forward and one back!

... I, like you, doubt the left-hand-drive story, and certainly there are no holes to hold the steering column on the left side of the dashboard frame. I cannot see Jowett changing the basic structure. Also, the dashboard is wood veneered, unique to the car. They would have had to remake the whole thing; I cannot accept that.... I have written to Mr. Cheetham and have just had a reply. He is, so far, the most reliable 'witness'. He confirms that there was no seating behind the driver, in spite of such a claim from our lady first owner. He confirms the wooden dashboard and also reminds me of the chassis support braces. These were the same sort of thing as fitted to the pre-war long chassis tourers. The same arrangement can be observed on railway coaches and a certain type of bridge!

I had assumed that these had been fitted later, in an attempt to support the rotting under-frame. But it seems these were fitted from new. I expect they took, hopefully, the place of the missing roof, so will have to be re-installed! He also advises caution with the hydro-mechanical brakes, which he reckons were not up to much. Having some experience with them I have converted the car to full hydraulic. I would think it better to do this to a car of such rarity. I would hate to bang it into something after all this time!

The Jowett Car Club held its millennium rally in Pitlochry, Scotland, in May 2000, which was a great success. My wife, Jane, and I arrived at the hotel on the Friday afternoon and settled into our room. Later in the evening, in the pouring rain, Dennis and Cath pulled up in front of the hotel in the Javelin convertible. This was one of its first trips out after finally finishing the car. Needless to say, Jane and I went straight out to see it, as this was the car that I had coveted for the previous twenty years or so. After a good look around the car, Dennis let me sit in the driver's seat, which was a real thrill.

The following day, I was watching the Jowetts arriving on the rally field, when I saw Dennis and Cath arriving in the convertible. Dennis pulled up next to me and asked me if I would like to drive it into position on the other side of the rally field. Did I want to? Definitely! I got into the car, praying I would not stall it, and drove it across the field, which has to be one of my greatest Jowett moments since I joined the club over thirty-seven years ago.

Sadly, the car has rarely been seen out and about since then, as mechanical problems and health problems have beset Dennis since then. In one letter, he wrote: 'I am still fighting to finish this albatross of a car, it is so badly built that it takes more time than a real car!'

Dennis wrote an article for the February 2003 issue of *The Jowetteer*, describing the car, which made very interesting reading:

I have always considered the Javelin to be more rigid than the Jupiter and it ought to have been campaigned more. About the drophead Javelin: this vehicle was created, as you know, in 1948 and shown at the 1948 Motor Show priced at £959.1.8d. The press gave it a good reception, but that was its last appearance! Quite why Jowett thought they could go down the drophead coupe road I can't think.

Carlton is said to have built it, although *Nick Walker's A–Z car British Coachbuilders* says they made no bodies after 1939.The entry for Carlton in *Who's Who of the Motor industry* (1965) mentions cars and commercial work? As a respected coachbuilder from 1925 working on better class cars, the Jowett does them no credit, even if it was, as it was said, a 'rush job'.

The top of the saloon was hacked off, as if by a butcher, along the waistline, and the B-posts were removed completely in the process. New posts were fitted further back. These were chunks of oak screwed to the long one-piece sills. Captive nuts inserted into the oak took two-quarter inch bolts each side from under these sills.

The lump of oak ran from 'B's to 'C's at waist level and planks covered the sills where the rear doors had been, with more oak on the C-posts and a cross bar to support the hood between them. All of this timber is held by wood screws - no brackets at all. Between the B-posts is an 'X' brace half-inch round bar across the car, screwed top and bottom with wood screws, and one piece of aluminium skin is swaged over the beetle back and down to sill level, closing what were the door apertures. The enormously heavy front doors, lengthened and filled with yet more oak, hang on the wooden B-posts. Oak frames the hole for the dickey seat lid and supports the boot lid hinges.

That is it—no strengthening is applied anywhere in the car! The thing was badly rotted when I found it yet the doors still shut and it was not sagging! At one time a brace had been fixed to the undersides of the chassis— I can't recall the technical term for it (Bentleys had it in the twenties)— this had rusted away. Now, when jacked up, it does not twist, and the doors remain true. It hasn't gone far due to gearbox problems, but on Edinburgh's shocking roads it rides well with no scuttle shake.

To bring the story up to date, we need to fast-forward fifteen years to November 2018. The Jowett Car Club had a stand at the Classic Car Show at the NEC, which was organised by the Midland Section of the Club, headed by the club president, Malcolm Oliver. As it was the seventieth anniversary of the 1948 Motor Show, they decided on an ambitious plan to try and re-create this first post-war show.

The cars on the 1948 stand were a black Javelin, a turquoise Javelin with the Perspex roof with a sun excluding roller blind over the front seat, the Javelin drop head coupé, a Javelin saloon in section, and an engine and gearbox in section. They had no problems in finding a black Javelin, but they were not able to find a turquoise Javelin, and certainly not one with the Perspex sunshine roof, as the 1948 car was one of only two produced.

The big problem was trying to arrange the transport of the Javelin drophead from Scotland to the show. Dennis was in poor health and had not worked on the car for some time and was a non-runner. The car had to be able to start, as it would have to be able to drive from the trailer into the NEC under its own power. This proved to be a monumental effort by club members, Eddie Hawthorne and Drummond Black, to get the Javelin drop head coupé to be able to drive into the NEC under its own power. A complete Jupiter, a Jupiter rolling chassis, and a vintage Jowett also appeared on the 2018 display.

The stand achieved runner up in the best themed club stand in the *Classic and Sportscar* awards. Nick Larkin, the motoring correspondent, also listed this as one of his 'top ten of cars' at the show in a lengthy article for *Classic Car Weekly*, which was thoroughly deserved in my opinion.

We were mentioned in glowing terms at the awards ceremony, a fantastic effort considering there were over 300 club stands and 3000 cars on display. Sadly, Dennis died in late 2019—a great loss to myself and the club.

Two views of the Convertible Javelin that appeared in *The Motor* magazine of 27 October 1948. It was listed as: 'Drop-Head Coupé £750 plus British Purchase Tax £209 1*s* 8*d*'. This was in fact the only prototype built, as the car never reached production. (*The Motor*)

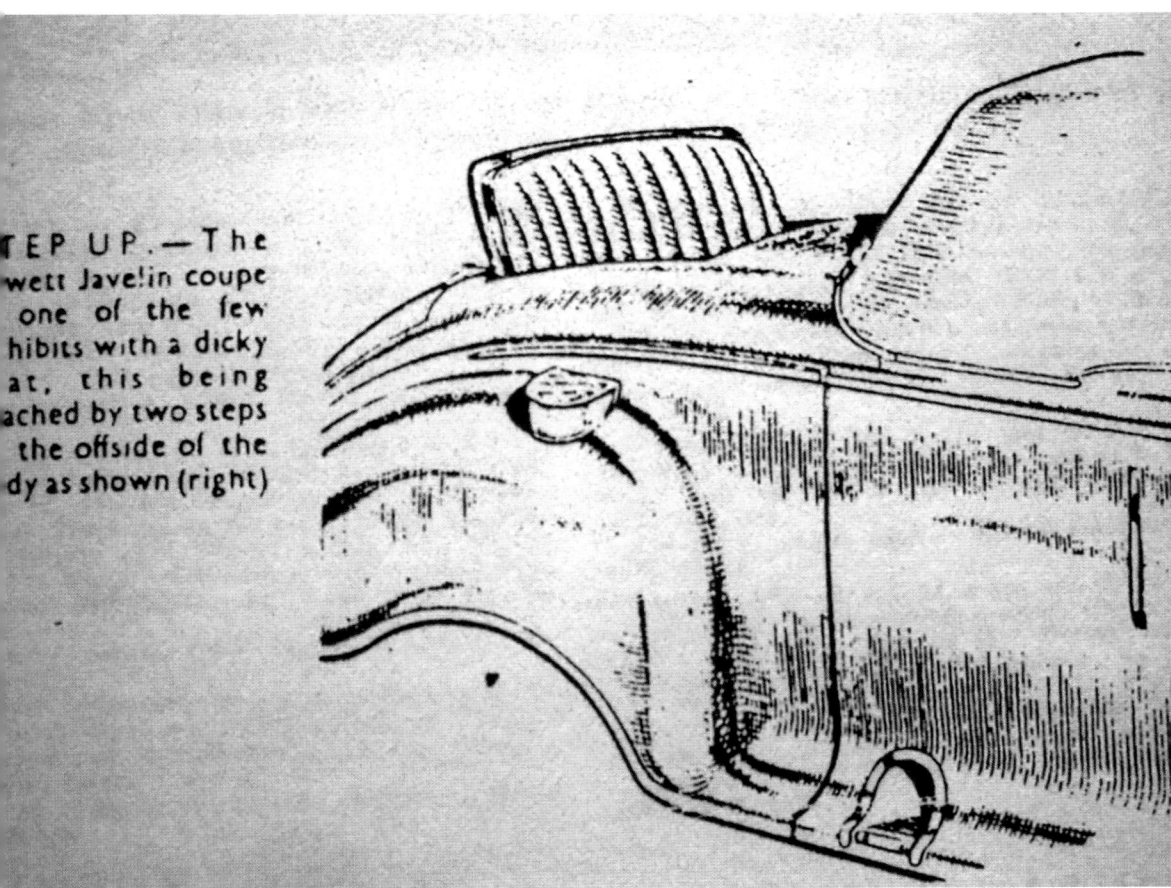

TEP UP.—The
wett Javelin coupe
one of the few
hibits with a dicky
at, this being
ached by two steps
the offside of the
dy as shown (right)

A drawing from *The Motor* magazine of 3 November 1948 shcwing the steps up to the dickey seat at the rear of the car. (*The Motor*)

Above and below: The car was first registered to the Jowett Ltd on 27 May 1949. It was then registered to the Jowett agents, Law Sons & Dean of Rochdale, on 10 April 1952. These pictures show Mr and Mrs Law at the wheel.

Above and below: The car was sold to Joan Wolstenholme as a twenty-first birthday present for her on 21 July 1956.

The car then was purchased by Ronald Bartram on 14 January 1959. This picture was taken in the early 1960s, by which time it was in very poor condition.

Opposite above: In 1965, the remains of the car were bought by Dennis Cremer, who then set about a very long and difficult restoration of the car.

Opposite below: Dennis Cremer arriving at the Jowett Car Club rally at Pitlochry in May 2000, the car's first trip out after its restoration.

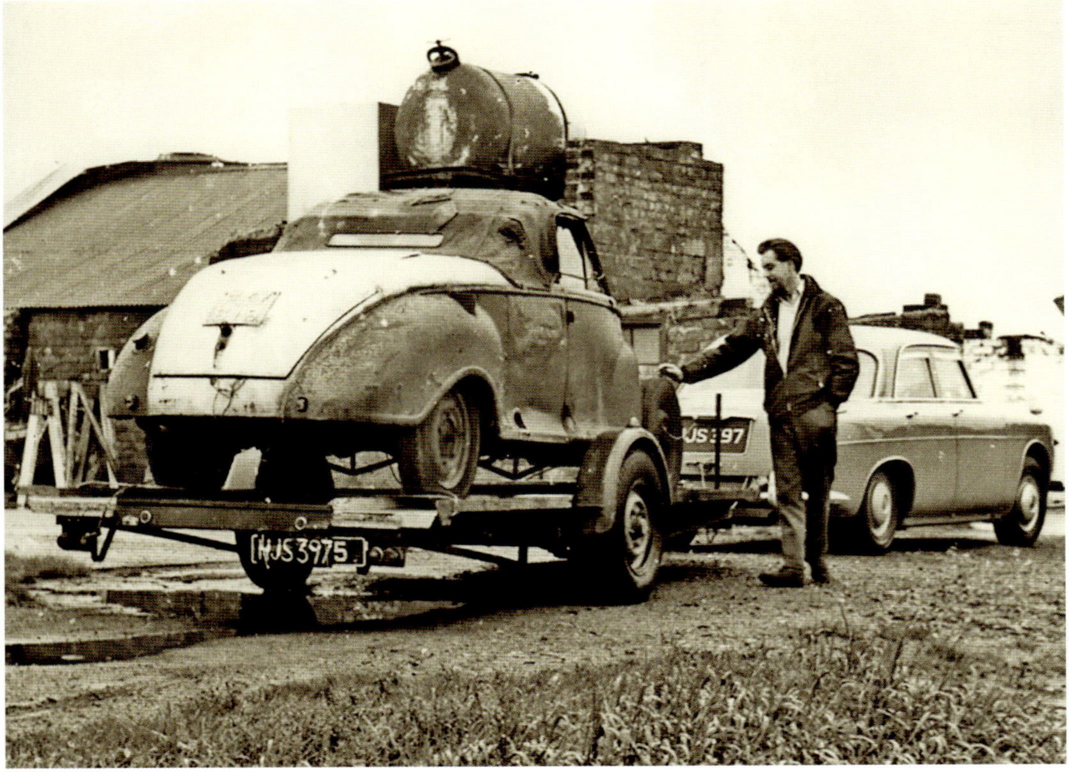
HJS 3975

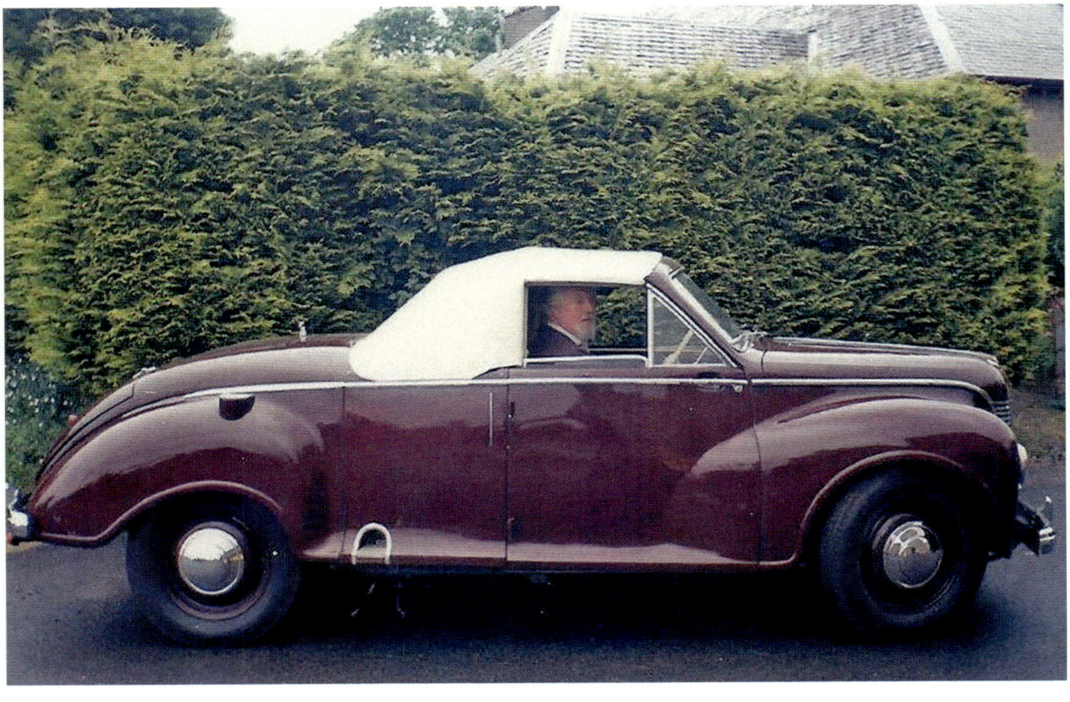

Two more views of the car at the Jowett Car Club rally at Pitlochry in May 2000.

The 1948 Javelin convertible at the Classic Car Show at the NEC in November 2019, voted as one of the stars of the show.

12

1949
ERA JAVELIN

T IS WELL documented that Prof. Eberan von Eberhorst of ERA designed the Jupiter chassis for Jowetts as Lesley Johnson, who controlled ERA, had suggested to Jowetts that following the success of the Javelin, there was the potential for an all-out sports car using Javelin mechanicals.

Only one ERA Javelin was bodied by ERA, but the design was not acceptable to Jowetts. Sadly, it would appear that the ERA Javelin has been lost to us. I spent many hours researching what could have happened to the car without success, but I had a breakthrough after being told that some Javelins had been used by the Metropolitan Police. Naturally, I wrote to the Met's archive department, who were very helpful. I was eventually sent a copy of a book that the Met had produced in the early 1970s, with the proceeds going to the Police Orphans' Fund (it is not dated) which was called *History of the Traffic Department of the Metropolitan Police*. It had an appendix at the back listing all the cars used by various departments of the Metropolitan Police right up to 1969.

This appendix did confirm that Javelins had been used. In 1947, the superintendent's department took delivery of a Javelin, but more interestingly, in 1950, they also took delivery of another Javelin and a Jowett ERA 1½-litre Saloon. The records show that the later Javelin and the ERA Javelin were transferred across to the police driving school in Hendon in 1955. Sadly, both cars were disposed of by them in 1957, and as far as I am aware, this was the last record of the car. I did have a request for information published in the Met's in-house magazine, *The Spotlight,* but sadly this did not produce any new leads.

Another snippet about the car came by way of a picture of it in *The Automobile* magazine from January 2000 in their 'Mystery Car' competition. It read:

> While researching Jonathan Wood's recent feature on Jowett in his best of British series, we came across this mystery car. The caption was entitled 'Exciting New Britisher' and detailed a new ERA Javelin which was to be featured at the Motor Show on stand 151. Did it ever make it there? Were in fact any made at all? We certainly don't know of any—do you?

A reply to this request came from the motoring journalist, David Venables in the April 2000 issue under the heading 'Jupiter Background':

With reference to your query about the ERA-Javelin in the January issue, this should have been on the Jowett stand at the 1949 Motor Show. The car was not finished when the show began, and I believe it was excluded by an SMMT rule that additional exhibits could not be added to stands after the start of the show.

It was finished during the first week of the show and then exhibited at Jowett's showroom in Albemarle Street, off Piccadilly. I went to see it. It is the car shown in your illustration. It had been quickly sprayed in a light metallic red and had not been polished and was quite rough. I seem to recall that there was no interior trim. Alongside was a bare chassis.

Visitors were asked to complete a questionnaire expressing their views about the car, and I remember that one of the questions asked if the bodywork was attractive. I gave an enthusiastic affirmation, as it was much better looking than most of the current British sportscars. I was very disappointed when it went into production about six months later as the Jupiter, which was rather prosaic by comparison with the ERA coupé.

I believe the car was designed by Eberan von Eberhorst, one of the pre-war Auto-Union team, assisted by David Hodkin, in the drawing office at Dunstable as a design exercise for Jowett. Soon afterwards, von Eberhorst went off to Aston Martin to design the DB3 chassis, while Hodkin stayed at ERA and used some of the principles of the ERA-Javelin chassis in the G-Type ERA, which later became the basis for the Type 450 Bristol.

I have to say, I found this very interesting as I did not know that the ERA Javelin was destined for the 1949 Motor Show but missed it by a week. Beauty is, as they say, is in the eye of the beholder, and clearly David Venables liked the ERA design better than the 'rather prosaic' final Jupiter design created by Reg Korner, Jowett's in-house designer. I must confess, I did not find the ERA Javelin attractive from the illustrations I have seen, but David had the advantage of seeing the car properly. I can honestly say that I much preferred Reg Korner's design, but obviously, it is personal choice.

What a difference a week makes—had the ERA Javelin been ready a week earlier, it would have been on display on the Jowett stand in 1949. If the questionnaire been on display with it and received favourable customer comments, this car could possibly have gone into production and the Jupiter, as we know it, would never have been built.

The car was greeted with great enthusiasm by the motoring press, this is what they had to say about it:

The Autocar, 30 September 1949: An ERA Javelin

Jowett and ERA Combine to Produce an Inexpensive High-Performance Car

Among the many new models introduced by the British Industry since the war there have been few small sports cars of modern design and appearance. Purchase Tax, rationing and the reduced standard of living have seriously curtailed the home market, and even though there is a brisk export markets, it has been difficult to guarantee sufficient sales to ensure an attractive selling price. The difficulty has been dramatically solved by Jowett Cars Ltd and Mr. Lesley Johnson who controls ERA Limited, resulting in the production of a most attractive 1½-litre sports car that will be known as the ERA-Javelin.

The car will be offered as a chassis or with a range of modern coachwork and will be marketed and serviced through Jowett agents throughout the world. The main mechanical components of the Javelin suitably adapted are incorporated into a new tubular chassis built by ERA Ltd. Already the Javelin saloon has gained important competition successes and incorporation of its well-tried engine, transmission and suspension units in a sports chassis evolved from the vast knowledge of the ERA organisation and designed under the supervision of Prof. Eberan von Eberhorst, is a guarantee of performance, roadholding and reliability. The use of mechanical units which are already in production for the Javelin saloon brings important savings in manufacturing costs and assures the owner of a full supply of spares at reasonable prices.

The chassis is a particularly clean design and study of the details shows many remarkable examples of ingenuity in adapting standard Javelin parts to avoid the production of special units which would increase cost without increasing efficiency. The frame is built up from straight lengths of mild steel tube of 2mm wall thickness and is designed to possess adequate rigidity in itself without any help from the body structure, thus leaving the owner free to use the lightest sports bodywork without fear of distortion under hard use. Bends have been avoided and the structure is built up entirely from straight lengths of tube. The main side members are three inches in diameter and are stiffened by an ingenious cruciform bracing amidships, consisting of four lengths of tube joined together with vertical stiffening plates welded above and below the junction. This part of the structure carries a centre bearing for the split propeller-shaft. As the forward part of the propeller-shaft does not rise or fall with the rear axle, the tunnel to cover it is barely noticeable on the floor of the driving compartment, despite the low build of the chassis.

The lower wishbones of the Javelin front suspension are pivoted in lugs which are secured to the main chassis tubes by bolts passing through small tubular inserts welded in. Support for the upper wishbones is provided on an extension built up from steel plate and two-inch diameter tubes, which also carries the radiator, steering and toe boards. The power unit is basically the well-known Javelin flat-four of 1,486cc but various small modifications have enabled the power output to be increased to approximately 60bhp. Larger Zenith carburettors are fitted, slight modifications have been made to the fairing of inlet and exhaust ports, and copper-lead bearings on steel shells have been substituted for standard white metal in the big-ends and front main bearings.

The steering gear is mounted over the gearbox and the layout has been considerably simplified. A new rack and pinion layout has been used, but the steering column and pinion from the normal Javelin pinion and selector gear have been retained, so that the only new parts required are the rack and tubes in which it slides. On the ends of the rack are ball joints connected to two short track rods engaging with the standard steering arms. This layout cuts out several joints and connections in the steering assembly and helps to reduce friction. There is an interesting damper in the steering consisting of two Mintex pads carried on a bolt that passes through a slot in the rack. The pads are spring loaded and grip the rack to provide a damping actin which is easily adjustable. Adjustment for mesh between the rack and the pinion is made by mounting the pinion in an eccentric bush.

Another feature of the steering gear is an exceptionally simple adjustment for the rake of the steering column. The tube carrying the rack is secured by two rubber rings sandwiched between conical faces on the outside of the tube itself and on the mountings welded to the chassis frame. The pressure on these mounting faces can be released by a screw adjustment, and after the bracket holding the column at the facia end has been slackened off the rack can be rotated to its new position. The setting of the track rods is quite unaffected, as they are attached to the balls at the ends of the rack, which simply rotate about their own centres.

The gearbox incorporates the higher second and third gear now that it is an optional extra on the Javelin and the high final drive ratio ensures effortless high-speed cruising.

The front suspension follows the normal Jowett layout with torsion bars and swinging arms but has an anti-roll bar clipped under the chassis frame and connected to the suspension by ball-ended links. The rear axle is carried on trailing arms connected by transverse torsion bars and located by a Panhard rod, rubber-cushioned at each end. There is also an anti-sway bar at the rear, neatly carried between two torsion bars and with its ends running parallel to the trailing links.

There are four body mounting points on each side of the chassis. The first is on a tubular cross-member ahead of the engine, carrying also the front bumper. The second is on the tubular extension which carries the wishbones for the front suspension. The third mounting which comes in the region of the door pillar, is on a tubular outrigger and the fourth is at the base of the swan-neck extension just forward of the rear axle. For bodies which have long tapering tails, a rubber girder extension can be added at the rear of the chassis frame to give additional support. The size, shape and capacity of the fuel tank, and the spare wheel mounting are also variable at the discretion of the owner or his coachbuilder. The plentiful body supports are intended to give the coachbuilder maximum assistance in providing a light body structure. The radiator is lower and wider than the Javelin unit, and the position of the fan has been dropped in order to permit a lower bonnet line. In front of the main radiator there is an oil cooler which increases the car's capacity for sustained speed.

The chassis costs £495 and is exhibited at the Jowett stand at the London Show. Meanwhile prototype bodies are being developed, and the first of these, an attractive sports coupé with luggage accommodation adequate for long Continental tours, is to be seen at the Jowett showrooms in Albemarle Street, London.

Motor Sport, October 1949

To the enthusiast the new ERA-Javelin fast touring chassis will be of the greatest appeal. It comprises the well-tried Javelin engine and main chassis components in a new tubular frame, the chassis assembled at ERA's Dunstable works to Jowett's order and marketed and serviced throughout the world by Jowett main agents. Prof. von Eberhorst, of Auto-Union fame, now ERA Chief Engineer, has played a large part in the design of the ERA-Javelin. More power has been obtained from the 72.5×90mm 1,486cc engine by installing an ERA-designed camshaft, while the latest Javelin lead-bronze main bearings and a full-flow oil filter-cum-radiator are used. The light-weight chassis is of 3-inch diameter tubes, running straight, and cruciform-braced and triangular-strutted to give rigidity. The wheelbase is 7 feet 9 inches against the Javelin's 8 feet 6 inches, and the front track being 4 feet 3 inches and that at the back being 4 feet 1 inch. The propeller-shaft has been modified to suit high speeds and anti-roll stabilisers front and back enable normal springing to be used, in conjunction with heavy-duty Woodhead Monroe shock-absorbers. The gear ratios are 4.1, 5.63, 8.91 and 14.62 to 1 against standard ratios of 4.86, 7.31, 11.6 and 18.9 to 1, while 5.50 instead of 5.25 tyres are fitted to the 16-inch pressed steel wheels. Prototype bodies are being developed, but this intriguing new ERA-Javelin will be exhibited as a chassis, the price of which is £495.

In addition, a normal and a de-luxe will be on stand 151, backed by a sectioned saloon, a sectioned engine and a working model of the clever Javelin torsional rear suspension.

Remembering the fine show, a Javelin saloon put up in winning the touring class in the Spa-24 Hour Race, there should be a bit of a jam around these particular British exhibits.

Jowett Cars Limited, 48 Albemarle Street, London W1.

Motor Sport, November 1949: Rumblings

The announcement of a new tubular-chassis high-performance version of the well-established Jowett Javelin, to be built by E.R.A. and powered and serviced by Jowett, was one of September's greater excitements. The new car, rightly called the E.R.A. Javelin, was displayed to a gathering of Pressmen at Jowett's Albemarle Street showrooms on September 27th, after which a cheery luncheon celebration was staged at Brown's Restaurant.

This E.R.A.-Javelin interested us very much indeed, for at last Motor Sport's plea for a lightweight British tubular-chassis high-performance car seemed to have been answered, although the engine is of 1,500 c.c., whereas 1,100 c.c. is effectively employed in such chassis on the Continent.

Indeed, this new Jowett seemed so promising at this preview that we were led to remark that at Earls Court it ought to be labelled clearly: 'THIS IS A BRITISH CAR,' in case foreign visitors glanced at it and passed it by, as something they must have seen at Turin and Paris! But our interest was more keenly aroused when we discovered that, far from E.R.A. Ltd. merely contracting to design and build the chassis for Jowett, the car is a personal interest of Leslie Johnson himself. He told us he is determined to produce a British car capable of competing with modern high-performance small Continentals and that, as far as chassis-testing can tell, he thought his objective had been achieved.

Its chassis price of £495 seems modest in the extreme and, while we prefer to reserve judgment until we have driven this exciting new car, Leslie Johnson's interest in its well-being suggests that Britain now has a car able to compete on level terms with the best of the small, high-performance Continentals, incidentally, thanks to a German engineer. For we owe the E.R.A.-Javelin's design to Prof. Dr Ing. Eberan von Eberhorst, late of Auto-Union and today Chief Engineer to E.R.A. Ltd.

As we were discussing this brilliant new chassis with Johnson, the prototype coupé made its entry on the showroom lift, amongst the assembled journalists. It had been sprayed only the night before, but so trim, so refreshingly different did the car look, prompting thoughts of Simca, Cisitalia, F.I.A.T., that those privileged to set eyes on the first complete E.R.A.-Javelin were captivated. We asked Johnson who was responsible for the body styling, and he said that no one person had designed it but that some years ago he brought from Italy the drawings of a F.I.A.T. coupé that had taken his fancy, declaring that one day he would build just such a body. The prototype E.R.A.-Javelin three-seater coupé is the result. It is daring in conception, with its all-enveloping style, sunk lamps, low air-entry, and high, rounded roof, terminating in a comparatively low tail incorporating a shallow luggage boot.

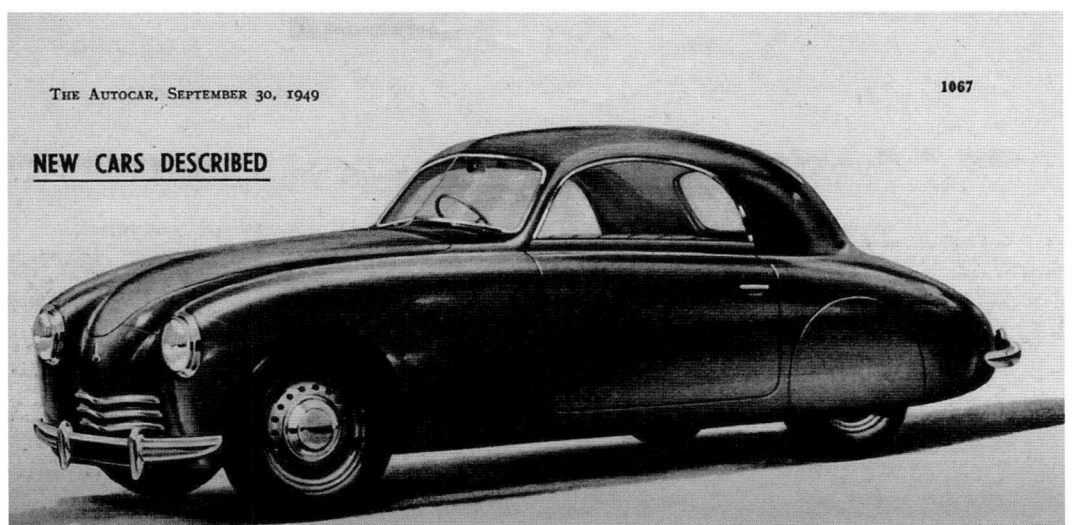

THE AUTOCAR, SEPTEMBER 30, 1949
1067
NEW CARS DESCRIBED

The 1949 ERA Javelin. (*The Autocar*)

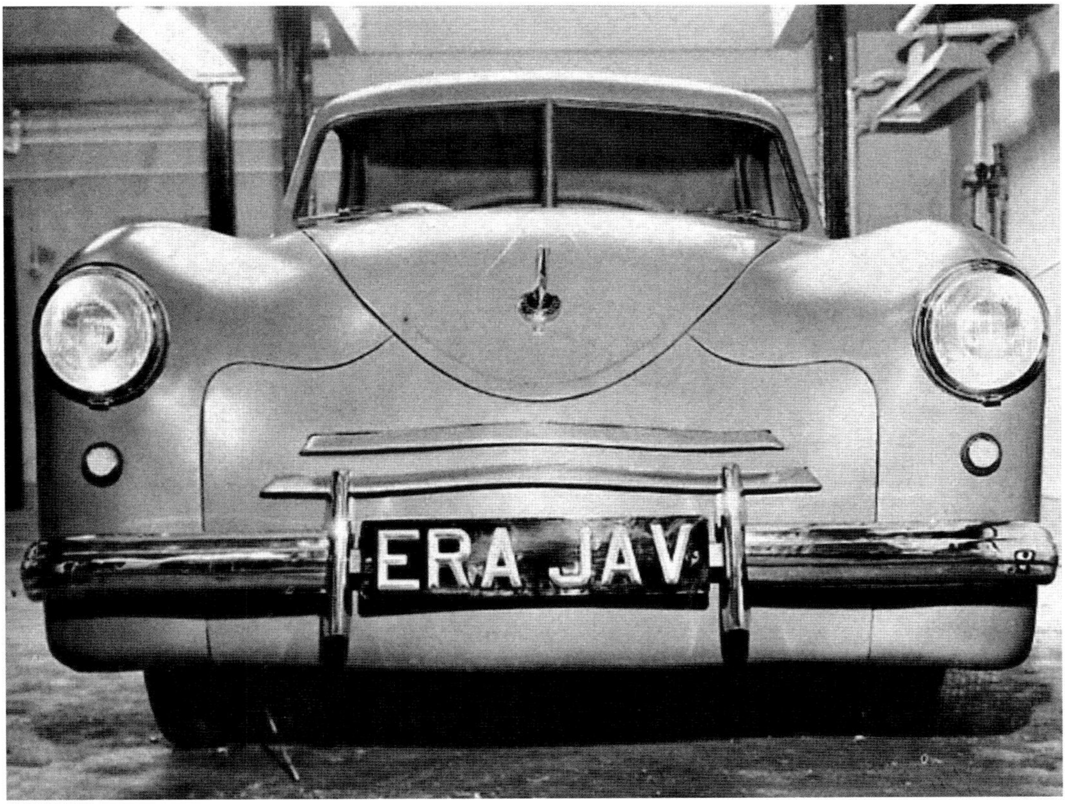
ERA JAV

Sketch of the ERA Javelin. (*The Autocar*)

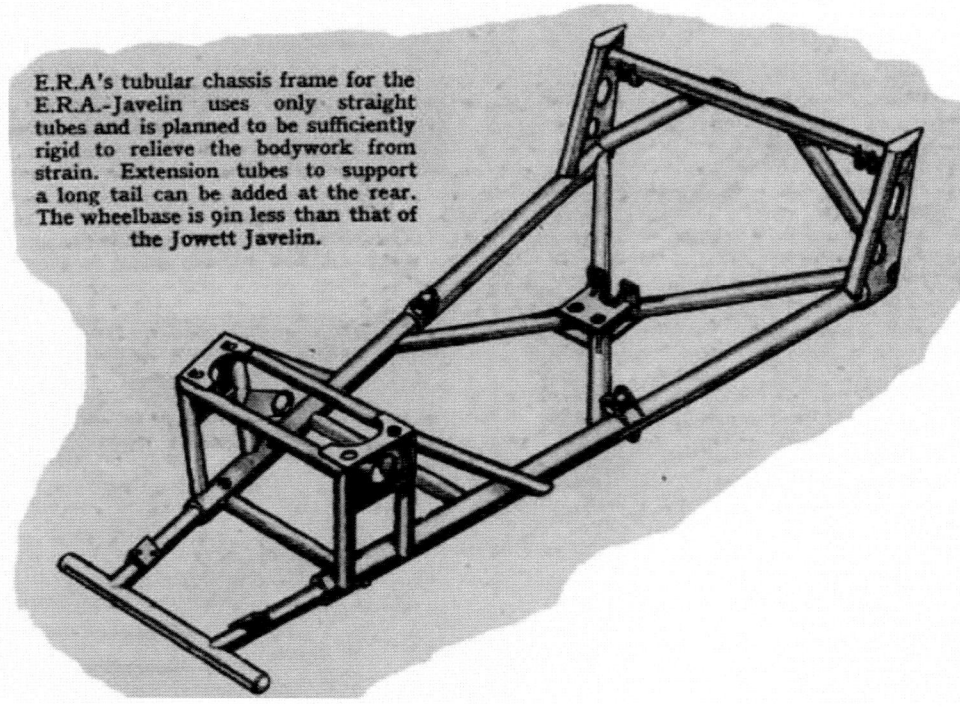

E.R.A's tubular chassis frame for the E.R.A.-Javelin uses only straight tubes and is planned to be sufficiently rigid to relieve the bodywork from strain. Extension tubes to support a long tail can be added at the rear. The wheelbase is 9in less than that of the Jowett Javelin.

E.R.A.-JAVELIN SPECIFICATION

Engine.—4 cyl, 72.5×90 mm, 1,486 c.c. Flat four with overhead valves operated by push rods. Two Zenith downdraught carburettors. Compression ratio 7.2 to 1. 60 b.h.p.

Transmission.—Single-plate clutch. 4-speed gear box with synchromesh on second, third and top. Ratios, 4.1, 5.63, 8.91 and 14.62 to 1. Hypoid bevel axle.

Suspension.—Front, independent with longitudinal torsion bars and anti-roll bar. Rear, normal axle with trailing arms, transverse torsion bars and anti-roll bar. Heavy duty telescopic dampers.

Brakes.—Lockheed hydraulic.

Wheels and Tyres.—Perforated steel disc wheels. 5.50×16in tyres.

Main Dimensions.—Wheelbase 7ft 9in, track (front) 4ft 3in; (rear) 4ft 11in.

Price.—Fast touring chassis £495. Purchase tax according to bodywork. Standard range of coachwork to be announced later.

Above: Sketch of the ERA Javelin chassis. (*The Autocar*)

Left: Specification of the ERA Javelin. (*The Autocar*)

13

1950
Yeoman

THE YEOMAN WAS not a vehicle that was built by Jowetts, but it has strong connections with them, as it was the brainchild of George Wansbrough, the director of Jowett Cars Ltd, and designed by Gerald Palmer, the Javelin designer. George thought that a Jowett of his own design could be a rival to the Land Rover in developing countries, such as Africa and India. This letter dated February 1989 from R. D. Wolstenholme, who was a neighbour of George, sets out the story; it is followed by Gerald Palmer's memories of this stillborn project:

It is probably not correct to say that the Yeoman was a car produced by Jowetts, but nevertheless, its connections with the Company are strong.

In the early 1950s a neighbour and close friend of the family was put in as Director of Jowetts by Lazard Brothers, the city financiers. His name was George Wansbrough and, until recently, lived near Winchester. Whilst my family was wondering whether they could afford a car at all (and ultimately just affording an ageing Bradford) George Wansbrough was the owner of a beautiful maroon Javelin, and thereafter became a car that I aimed to own until I finally succeeded in doing in 1967!

In the very early 1950s, George Wansbrough was considering his own design for a Jowett rival for the Land Rover. This vehicle was built in prototype, and I clearly remember jaunts with my father and George Wansbrough over large areas of unfenced common land in Hampshire as part of testing this revolutionary vehicle.

It consisted of a slab-fronted semi-triangular cab in which the driver sat perched well forward in the centre of the vehicle with all his instruments around him. Behind the driver (and rather like a fire engine) was a seat for three passengers. Behind the cab was a standard truck body with a floor roughly the same height as that of a standard rear engine Volkswagen truck. The engine was a modified Jowett Javelin unit [The original engine used was the twin-cylinder Bradford and not the four-cylinder Javelin engine] inserted from the rear of the vehicle and beneath the rear load platform but above the back wheels. The vehicle had very large wheels and the spare wheel mounted on the front vertical face of the cab. There was no left or right-hand drive version of the vehicle as the driver sat up front in the centre. The Wansbrough thinking behind the vehicle was that it should have good export potential.

It was thought that the vehicle could be built cheaply on the Sub-Continent, and it was designed so the engine could be very easily taken out and replaced with another (in aircraft fashion). The connection with aircraft is more than tenuous. Apparently, at one stage, there was a very real chance that the Royal Air Force would buy the vehicle on masse. It will be recalled that subsequently, the Air Force purchased a large number of Land Rovers with two-wheel drive only. That apparently was the market that Wansbrough was after, probably failed to get it due to the demise of the Jowett Company at a vital stage of negotiations with the Air Ministry.

Although aged only 6 or 7, I recall clearly being taken to school in this vehicle and testing its load-carrying capacity over some of the roughest heathland in the County.

George Wansbrough was more of a concept man than an engineer (that is presumably why he was put in as Director by a Finance Company) and I never forget my father achieving quite an unwarranted a reputation as an Engineer when he managed to restart the failed Javelin engine by simply soaking up the water which had accumulated around the sparking plug wells. In fact, like the early Javelins, it was almost necessary to remove the engine from the vehicle in order to change the sparking plugs.

I cannot recall what finally happened to this famous prototype Yeoman, but I rather think it was ultimately 'cannibalized' by the family following the demise of the Jowett Company. Some years after that, George Wansbrough went on to become instrumental in the launching of the luxury Gordon Keeble car.

Thinking about my early childhood amongst Jowetts and my subsequent aspirations to own these wonderful vehicles, leaves me wondering what happened to my initially white, but subsequently red Jowett Jupiter registered RTD111. Does anyone know what happened to my previous Javelin registered NAH842, or even my family's Bradford van registered MPO859?

R. D. Wolstenholme

I am pleased to say that the Jupiter registered RTD111 (chassis number 646) is alive and well, but sadly, there is no trace of the Javelin and Bradford.

Gerald Palmer's account of the Yeoman project follows:—

The interesting letter from R D Wolstenholme about the Jowett Yeoman prompts me to pick up my pen and write to you about this project in which I was heavily involved. In fact, I designed the vehicle for George Wansbrough to his specification.

It emerged from the visit he made to India in about 1950 on behalf of H M Government to report on the economic development of that country and for road transport. He considered that instead of producing a conventional passenger car, as they were doing, what was needed was a simple vehicle capable of carrying 5 or 6 humans and 10cwt of rice. It would also be capable of light land tillage and other agricultural duties. It was to be of very simple construction involving the minimum expenditure on production tooling which would be locally made. The only units made at a central source, i.e. the UK, being the engine and transmission. Wansbrough saw a market for such a vehicle, not only in India, but also most developing countries.

The salient feature of the design was that the whole platform area of the vehicle was used for passengers or cargo, unlike the Land Rover, for example, where the engine cover accounts for over a third of the area. The engine was at the rear under the cargo floor and it was here that the Bradford engine was the obvious choice due to its low height. This then was the Jowett connection, and I believe that Wansbrough put the project to the Jowett Board of Directors who rejected it. However, he obtained finance from a private source and a prototype was designed by the well-known freelance designer named Sampriento and built by Thomson & Taylor at Brooklands track. Wansbrough was dissatisfied with the result and sought my opinion, I told him the vehicle was far too complicated, difficult to assemble and too costly, and I could not see it fulfilling the role that he had in mind. 'Will you design me another?' he asked, and that is how I became involved.

It was done in my spare time whilst designing cars for MG and Riley and meant many nocturnal visits to Brooklands where the vehicle was being built under the supervision of the redoubtable Ken Taylor, with whom I soon established an excellent rapport. The design was simple to the point of being crude, the frame and all sheet metal parts could be made on a bending press, the front independent springing was by two transverse leaf springs and the rear swing axle had half elliptic springs augmented by a transverse leaf spring for maximum load. A simple 4-speed gearbox cum final drive with a lockable differential was built with the Bradford engine behind the rear axle. This vehicle shown in the photographs was extensively tested over very rough terrain and farmland in Hampshire and no doubt is the one in which Mr. Wolstenholme rode.

With very low gear ratio, a lockable diff and preponderance of weight on the rear driving wheels it could extricate itself from the muddiest holes and at the same time was quite comfortable on the highway. It soon became apparent, however, that the Bradford engine was not powerful enough. Wansbrough therefore replaced it with a V4 air-cooled Petter unit which greatly improved its performance.

Not having the capability to manufacture the Yeoman (for such it was named himself) he demonstrated it to several of the established manufacturers of the day, but he could not get anyone interested in the project. So, reluctantly he had to abandon it. Late in the programme I redesigned the vehicle using a Perkins108 diesel engine mounted ahead of the axle. Wansbrough was able to get the White Motor Corporation of the USA interested in this version and we gave a presentation of it to their Chairman in London. No prototype in this format was built and they finally turned it down.

This then is the story of the Jowett Yeoman; it was an interesting attempt to produce a basic transport for developing countries. In the ensuing years many other attempts have been made, including a study made into this problem by the United Nations, but none of them has been conspicuously successful.

What a shame that this venture was yet another example of a clever idea that ended up being a stillborn project, even though it had great potential for use in India and other developing countries.

Above, below, and opposite above: Three views of the 1950 Yeoman, designed by Gerald Palmer, the Javelin designer. (*Gerald Palmer*)

The very spartan interior of the Yeoman. (*Gerald Palmer*)

14

1951
BRADFORD CD RANGE

I WROTE THIS ARTICLE for *The Vintage Commercial Vehicle* magazine, which appeared in their January–February 1989 issue. I have made a few minor alterations to the text as new information came available:

The Bradford CD was not Jowett's last-ditch attempt to produce a new range of vehicles, as is sometimes thought, since the actual designs were drawn up as early as the beginning of 1951.

The idea was to enable a whole range of vehicles to be manufactured using as many of the same body panels as possible. The intention was to produce a two-door saloon car, a pick-up, van and estate car. The size of the vehicles was to be a good deal bigger than the existing Bradford van and more in line with the dimensions of the Standard Vanguard van produced around that time.

The first prototype earned the nickname of 'The Tram' on account of three rows of two seats all facing forward with folding seat squabs like those on trams. The body of this vehicle was built in the Experimental Department of the Jowett factory in Idle and not by Briggs. It had four doors with no opening rear, whereas the final CD range had two rear opening doors but only two side doors. It differed in various other ways, for example, the front grill was markedly different from the final design. It was registered GKY510.

Only one saloon was ever produced, a two-door model registered JKU399, it shared the same front end as the estate cars, with a grille reminiscent of the Jenson bodied Austin A40 Sports and the front wings bearing a striking resemblance to the MK1 Ford Consul. It has been suggested that the front wings are in fact the same as the Consul, which would indicate that after Jowett's closure the tooled-up production line for the CD at Briggs was used in part by the new owners.

After the closure of the Jowett factory the CD car, together with the pick-up and estate cars and vans went to Howden Clough, where Jowett Engineering Ltd continued making spares and servicing Jowetts for the next ten years. At the closure of Jowett Engineering Ltd in 1964, it is said that the pick-up and one of the estate cars were sold as scrap to George Mitchell in Scotland, while the CD car was abandoned in a derelict state on its roof with most of the mechanicals stripped off it. It is assumed that this was eventually scrapped around this time.

The other vans and estate cars which went to Howden Clough were heavily tested and also used as JEL's workhorses and probably also scrapped during this 10-year period.

It is now thought that one car, one pick-up, six vans and six estate cars were built by Briggs, which excludes 'The Tram' built by Jowetts themselves. Four of the estate cars were exported to New Zealand.

Had the CD project got underway, it was quite likely that there would have been substantial problems with the new twin-cylinder engine which seemed unlikely to have been powerful enough for such a large body. The weight of the estate car was said to be just over a ton and the OHIV engine for the CD would have produced 27–30 bhp, compared with 25-bhp for the Bradford CC engine. As an experiment (or expedient), tests were carried out with the 4-cylinder Javelin engine installed, which apparently produced a satisfactory performance.

Interestingly three of the four CD estate cars which went to New Zealand still exist, one of these has been restored and is on the road, the other two are both in poor condition, but are basically complete and awaiting restoration. The fourth estate was also found in New Zealand in a semi-derelict state, with the bodywork too far gone for restoration. However, the chassis was restored, and a new body was fitted using a replica Jupiter bonnet, Morris Oxford doors and Javelin rear wings. The result is a very pleasing four-seater convertible.

The one CD estate left in the UK has recently been bought by a Jowett Car Club member in Essex who plans a complete rebuild. As the only surviving CD in Europe, it is clearly an important find and a key element in the history of the Jowett CD range.

Thirty-two years later, the UK CD has changed hands twice and has still not reappeared, which is a great shame. The restored CD in New Zealand was restored again a few years ago by the late Ray Win and is now on display in the Ray Win Museum in New Zealand along with his huge collection of other Jowetts. The other two CDs awaiting restoration in New Zealand are still waiting. Vic Morrison and his convertible (known as the CDR3) are still going strong and seen regularly at events etc in New Zealand—so not too much has changed.

The Jowett CD List Compiled by Alan Rushworth in August 1990

Updated by Noel Stokoe, June 2021

CD1 GKY540 was hand built at Idle using many Javelin parts, these included front and rear doors, windscreen & scuttle, front wings, lights & front bumper, wheels tyres & wheel trims. Utility without rear door. CC engine and hydro-mech brakes. Metallic grey and registered in January 1951. Known as the 'tram' because of the seats which were in three rows all facing forward with seat squabs like old trams. Fate unknown.

CD2 HKW272: First Briggs bodied utility from Dagenham, fitted with the new 32.5 BHP IOE twin engine, registered February 1952. It was involved in much testing including 12 weeks endurance test in the Dales from Feb to April. Also used abroad to Switzerland and back in LHD form. After these tests, a modified Javelin engine was fitted, and it was used by Phill Green on performance and cooling trials in London during the 1953 Motor Show. It was finished in pale blue and had a different door handle design to the later cars, similar to the Ford Consul type. CD2 & CD3 were the only ones to have 'Bradford' in script on the front panel. The lighting and horn stalk was different, and the fresh air ducting was only on CD2 as it didn't work well enough. It went to New Zealand late in 1953 with three other CD estates but was involved in an accident with a timber lorry there in 1955. Repaired using Zephyr front and bonnet. nearly scrapped in early 60s. Somehow survived but the body by now past redemption has been rebuilt with a homebuilt sports body using a Jupiter front. Morris Oxford MO doors and Javelin rear wings. Now known as CDR3 its NZ registration was LK 3635. This restoration/reincarnation was carried out by Vic Morrison, who still owns it and uses it regularly, its registration number is now CDR3.

CD3 HKY566: The only pick up made, was the nicest version of the whole CD range. Fitted with the IOE engine initially and a Javelin unit later. Colour was a pale grey-green, probably Ford Channel green and registered July 1952. Taken to Dagenham by Phil Green for seat tests and later retainer by Jowett Engineering and used as a service recovery vehicle. Bought by George Mitchell for a nominal. sum in the spring of 1964 who used it for some eighteen months on trade plates. The chassis was later sent for welding but inadvertently scrapped. The weathered remains, bonnet, one wing, door, part of cab and remains of front & tailgate recently were acquired by Tony Palmer.

Tony had picked up these panels when he was buying the Rawson-bodied Jupiter from George Mitchell in the late 1980s. Sadly, Tony died suddenly in 2002 in his fifties, which was a great blow to the Club. At the time of Tony's death, he was part-way through restoring the Jupiter, and planned to display the CD remains somehow. His two sons still own the Jupiter, but I understand that the CD panels may have been scrapped.

CD4 JKU399: the only saloon made. Originally proposed as a four door, six light, was in fact made as a two door four light saloon. In no way like the Javelin, a Brigg's design with Ford Consul type front wings, staid and ordinary to look at until you opened the door to see an unusual step-up to the floor inside. Quite a basic car with flat screen, slide down windows, exposed hinges all round and open glove boxes on the dash which was metal with central instrument panel. Two spoke steering wheel with straight horn/lighting stalk. Two separate front seats, not unlike older Bradford CC and the door trims were secured by countersunk self-tappers around the edge. Painted jade metallic green with cream wheels and brown interior. Registered March 1953 and was fitted with twin fuel tanks and the twin IOE engine which had twin carbs. Retained at Howden Clough and fitted with a Javelin engine & gear box, was used as a run about and seen around Batley. Eventually dumped upside down near the 'cottage' at the mill with mechanics removed in 1962 and presumably scrapped.

CD5 Not built.

CD6 Not built.

CD7 Not built.

CD8 Not built.

CD9 Not built.

The pre- production run hoped for in November 1952 did not materialise until the following spring when the debt to Briggs had been paid off. They were all estate/van shells, five of each according to Briggs paperwork recently discovered. The CD chassis was designed to take either the twin IOE, or Javelin 4 cylinder. A diesel had also been specified for it although the results of this were not very promising. The realisation that the IOE twin was just not powerful enough plus further development needed on the gearbox put things back somewhat. The CD estate is about the same size as a Mk1 Zephyr estate and a bit taller. Colours were Opal (grey), green and beige and the vans mainly black.

CD10 Grey Van registered JKU945, the sole CD survivor in the UK, was owned by Alan Rushworth in 1990, later sold to Frank Livesey. It was sold soon after to Simon Wood who started a full restoration, but we are still waiting to see it again after all this time!

CD11 Grey Van UK Registration number not known, NZ reg EW9022. A utility with the R4 type engine (a variant of the Javelin/Jupiter unit). Painted grey it was shipped to New Zealand in 1953, Completely rebuilt by M. Bergin in the late 1970s, later owned by Leo Boulter and painted maroon. It was sold to the late Ray Win, who restored it again and is now on display in the Ray Win Museum—the only restored example in the world.

CD12 Grey Van Registration not known.

CD13 Green Van Registration not known. No details except that it was a van, dark green, blue or black. Could have been the van in-Autocar picture (1958) registration JKW66 or JKW88. Was dumped in a stream near Howden Clough in 1963, still there in 1966.

CD14 Green Van Registration not known.

CD15 Green Van Registration not known.

CD16 Grey Estate Car Registration unknown.

CD17 UK Registration number not known. Utility, pale green with brown interior. Only survivor with IOE engine, but with a broken crank and one pot missing. Shipped to NZ in 1953 and stored many years now in need of complete restoration. NZ reg. is EW7071.

CD18 UK Registration number. not known. Utility or van with windows, metallic green, R4 engine. Only CD with opening quarter lights. Shipped to NZ in 1953, owned by a recluse who even threatened a New Zealand club member that he would destroy it if his name were published! Both CD17 & CD18 are still unrestored but are both being cared for by Neil Moore in New Zealand.

CD19 Not known.

CD20 Not known.

The missing CDs could be any of the following: JKW66 or 88, a van, black in *The Autocar* article on Jowett Engineering 1958 which could have been the CD used by employees as a works hack up to the end in 1963. This was dark in colour and had a bench seat fitted down both sides. JKW115 a van, engine, colour and chassis number unknown, photographed in 1953 and in another photo taken in 1958 at Howden Clough, then in black with side windows added. JKW 367 a utility, photographed in 1953 and then no details. Could have been the other CD that went to Brough (Blackburn Aircraft) with CD10 and scrapped there. LAK ... a utility, colour dark green seen being scrapped at Howden Clough in 1963. There was also a beige van seen at Howden Clough in 1959.

When I started researching into the CD Bradford range, I realised that very little seemed to be known about them by motoring journalists and club members. Much of the information that had been published in our club magazine, *The Jowetteer*, and motoring journals was incorrect, which is why I wrote the above piece in 1989. In his fascinating 1968 book entitled *The Cars That Got Away: Ideas, Experiments & Prototypes*, Michael Frostick is a typical example where he wrote the following:

This Jowett seems to be nameless and numberless (possibly type CD) and Jowetts themselves, although still in existence, can say no more than those details and drawings of this prototype, together with its technical data, have become misplaced or destroyed.

Because they have been out of production for ten years and have moved their address, we must thank Gordon Wilkins for a memory and these three pictures [one of each of the CD car, estate car and pick-up] where it transpires that this car range was to be a development of the Bradford van.

Using something which sprang basically from the Bradford engine (with Javelin heads and valve gear) fitted with a monocoque body/chassis using a 4-speed Javelin gearbox and what must be near enough Javelin suspension.

Looking now rather bulbous and Standard Vanguard-ish, the car was by the standards of its day fairly stylish, and if put on the market at a reasonably low figure, it might well have become a kind of British Volkswagen in terms of sluggish dependability and general usefulness. Wilkins remembers that it went 'quite well', and no doubt its handling qualities were as good as its more expensive brother, all of which adds up to one more reason to regret the coming of the Giants and the demise of the individual manufacturers.

It is one of the models which we are concerned about was one of those that remained for ever in the darkest corners of the pool. It may well have proved a turning point in the company's existence. Fate, however, was against such notions and all we can now do is record the glories of what might have been.

In 1985, I wrote a note for our club magazine, *The Jowetteer*, asking for information on the CD range, and several long-standing club members wrote with their reminiscences, but it was surprising as to how much some of these accounts varied. Phill Green wrote a very detailed account of how he test drove the CD Estate registered HKW272, which was published in my book, *My Car was a Jowett*, in 2003. I would have liked to use his article here, but it seems inappropriate to duplicate it here.

The CD car and pick-up, I can contribute the following—

CD Car—Was probably run by the factory after going to Batley. It was lying upside down without most of its mechanical parts outside a building called 'the cottage' in the factory grounds (at Howden Clough). Presumably scrapped by the factory.

CD Pick-Up—Was fitted with a Javelin engine and used as the factory work horse until 1963 when Jowett Engineering Ltd closed. The factory refused to sell it since it had never been on the market and hence, like the car, was liable for purchase tax, at the time this would have been unrealistic. It stood in the factory grounds after the premises had been vacated until about Easter 1964 when George Mitchell gave the caretaker £5.00 to take it away.

Somehow, he registered it and I think he ran it for a while before scrapping it—perhaps to salvage some CD parts. It is an interesting thought that the CD car is still at Howden Clough, but it was not a nice vehicle!

It is curious how memory plays tricks, but I am sure it was said that the IOE CD engine performed quite well but was unbearably rough and noisy. I recall a chap called Heaton, who was workshop boss at Howden Clough, claimed to have driven it on trials paced by an A30 and he said the CD performed better but the engine was unmarketable, and the problems were never solved. I also recall it being said that the installation of the Javelin engine was only a desperate measure because there was no prospect of selling the IOE. Still seems the experts do not now say that. Incidentally, the gearing of the CD was such that with the Javelin engine you could burn rubber off the back tyres! I did have a long ride in the CD van which I recall as quite comfortable, and it did perform well with the Javelin engine. It pulled well because we towed JAK 76 (Jupiter) on a low loader as if it didn't exist.

The point about the sale of the CD's was raised in reference to the pickup which George Mitchell wanted to buy. Purchase tax was levied on the cost of manufacture. That is if it cost £1000 to produce a CD prototype in 1952, Purchase Tax payable in 1965 would be a % of £1000, not of the then current price. So, a scrap vehicle might be worth only £5 (what GM gave eventually to the caretaker for the pick-up) but it would have been liable to £660 PT when that tax was at its peak. I think tax was 33.3% in the 1960s but what a fuss there would have been trying to estimate the manufacturing cost. The saloon was then quite within restorable limits but the way one saw it, it was an undistinguished tank of a thing which no-one would be remotely interested in. GM scrapped the pick-up whilst it was still a useable vehicle, with hindsight we know otherwise.

I believe the front wings actually were Ford ones or else were replaced by Ford units. It is quite likely JEL used the saloon around the factory, after all it was there 10 years.

Dr Harry Brierley, the club's technical information officer, sadly now deceased

In the winter of 1953 or 1954 a medium metallic green CD estate car was delivered to the experimental department of the Daimler Company in Coventry. It had Javelin badging on it and the interior was brown with separate front seats with a centre gearchange. The engine was removed and fitted to a dynameter in the engine test house. Testing was carried out for two to three weeks and the engine was then refitted. I do not recall any road-testing taking place. The object of the exercise was not very clear, but at that time the Daimler Co was taking a big interest in the all-aluminium engine from the Panhard from the period, and in fact they owned a light green example plus a large quantity of body parts. It may just be that upon the demise of Jowett, the Javelin engine was considered as an alternative to the Panhard twin should the Panhard be assembled here under license. This is pure conjecture as I have no evidence to support this theory. It is, however, a fact that Daimler were disappointed by the Javelin's engine performance, but why this should be I do not know as their own 1.6-litre Lanchester engine was of similar output. The car was returned to Bradford by a Daimler driver who was very impressed by its performance and ride quality.

John Box, long-term club member

I am 99% certain that the CD was never road tested by any motoring journal. The prototypes were produced in 1951 or 1952 but production was delayed for a number of reasons.

1 Lack of capital.
2 Need for further development of the twin engine.
3 Gearbox problems (the CD used the Javelin/Jupiter box in a different casing).

When car production ceased in 1953 Jowetts had paid the tooling bill to Briggs for the CD but were up to their necks with gearbox problems which meant that CD body/chassis units were not much use. Also, Jowetts reduced the Briggs order drastically and Briggs refused to play. With no Javelin bodies and the CD probably not quite developed the commercial viability of the concern was doubtful—the R4 alone (CD based) would not have kept the plant viable, and the CC Bradford would not compete with the new generation of 100E Fords, Minors and Austin A35s. Therefore, the money men on the board advised the shareholders to accept the offer for the plant from International Harvester and eventually the creditors received £1 for £1—Jowett did not go bust!

As to the fate of the vehicles, I understand that the saloon was broken up at Howden Clough in 1963. George Mitchell 'acquired' the pick-up (with Javelin engine) from the tip at Howden Clough in 1963 and later broke it up. He also owned one of the estates (Javelin engine) which is now for sale in Manchester. I believe, but I cannot substantiate that in all 12 pre-production prototypes were made, the rest going to New Zealand and of these at least two had the twin engine. Certainly, two survive, one in the original form and one rebodied as a sort of 4-seater Jupiter.

As to performance, I understand that with the 4-cylinder engine the vehicle was good for 80mph plus, whilst the twin (about 32bhp) was capable of giving the contemporary Austin A40 Devon van a good run for its money.

George Garside, long-term club member and author of a book on Jowetts

George Green (Jowett's sales director) remembers the CD. He gave it some test runs and said that it was grossly underpowered with the twin engine. He recalls also that the saloon had twin fuel tanks mainly due to their being of small size, so two gave a greater range for long distance testing. Two tanks would also create a better balance than one big one at one side.

Len Shackleton, who test-drove the CD, and Roy Lunn both concur that the twin was not powerful enough for the size of body intended. However, the project was designed to take either a twin or a Javelin type flat-four; in fact, the survivors here and in New Zealand have the four, apart from one of the New Zealand examples which is not on the road and has the original twin but with one cylinder missing.

CD Estate E3/CD/10 JKU945 by Alan Rushworth, *The Jowetteer*, February 1986

Although the rebuild of my Javelin is only half completed, the story of the CD estate, languishing in a garage up north with no sign of a taker saddened me. So, a phone call to Manchester and a promise of being collected at the other end saw me on the 8.15am to Altringham had decided a look at the one dismal day. I decided at least to take a look at the thing. Ted Allen met me at the station that June day in 1985 and soon we arrived at a row of lock ups as the rain started falling again. The doors opened and I was greeted with the back end of a large and rusty estate car. My first impression was of its size, it was much bigger than had imagined. It was filled up with its panels and much junk. Had it been merely and old Austin, Standard or whatever, would have just walked away, but because it was a Jowett, and the only surviving CD in the UK felt that something had to be done ... so I bought it.

The logbook shows it to be a Jowett Estate Car, chassis No E3/CD/10. It appears to be identical to Steve Wickens' in New Zealand (E3/CD/11), four CD estates were exported to NZ and three have survived. CD/2 is the special bodied one, CD/11 is Steve's with R4 type 4-cylinder engine, and CD/17 survives with its original twin cylinder IOE engine (minus one pot unfortunately). It is very sad that the pickup had not survived, rumour has it that the chassis was sent for shot blasting but due to some mix up was cut up for scrap.

The photos tell their own story! After many years of neglect, she is in pretty poor shape, the main areas for concern being gutters, both sides around wheel arches and the back end. The chassis is sound but the body having been stripped of paint is rusty. As mentioned earlier, she is quite large, length 14' 6", width 5' 7" and height 5' 10". The weight with Javelin engine was 19cwt with the twin it is 1-ton 63lbs. The front suspension is Javelin rubber bushed type and the rear is 12 leaf springs. 15" wheels fitted and its original colour was some sort of green, possibly metallic, but I cannot be sure. There is very little of its interior left. Door windows are push down type. The whole front is bolt on, the bodyshell being from bulkhead back.

According to the logbook, JKU 945 was first registered 7th May 1953 to Jowett Cars Ltd, the book being signed by Mr. Snell. The car went to Howden Clough and passed to Blackburn Aircraft Ltd on 6th November 1956. It was originally fitted with the twin IOE engine, but this was removed in 1958 (I wonder what became of this unit) when a Javelin engine was fitted along with a Javelin radiator and gearbox, the original battery position being altered to take the radiator. It passed on to a Mr Taylor of North Ferriby (just outside Hull) on 9 Nov 1961 and to George Mitchell of Cleish, Kinross on 9 August 1967. It would seem he was the last to drive the car, as the next owner, Allan Wright informed me that the engine/gearbox was missing when he bought the car. In fact, many other parts are missing including all engine ancillaries, radiator, seats and exhaust. The rear quarter bumpers and spare wheel cover panel disappeared many years ago when a tow bar was fitted.

Mr Wright stored the car under covers until Ted Allen bought it in 1978. He stripped it of paint and parts and rebuilt the base of the bulkhead on both sides, the front panel and restored a rear door. At present, (Nov '85) 'CiD' as we call her is lying dogo [sic.] in its kennel (as my wife calls it) at the bottom of our garden. The chassis and body were manhandled down the garden with the kind help of friends and neighbours. All parts have been liberally waxoyled pending further work.

Alan worked on the CD for several years, but eventually sold it to another club member, who in turn sold it on. It is now in the care of another club member who has a large collection of Jowetts. He continues with the restoration, but we are still waiting to see it in its restored state some thirty years later.

CD Utility E3/CD/11 in New Zealand by Keith Wear, *The Jowetteer*, September 2008

Ray Win is a member of our Club living in Nelson, in New Zealand's South Island. He has been retired for many years, having spent all his working life in the motor trade. As a young man he wanted to be a motor mechanic but at that time with no jobs immediately available, he asked around and was taken on at a firm of car wreckers. Ray says, 'It was the best thing that ever happened as I learned all the car parts, how to dismantle and clean them, and then to put them on the correct shelf.'

He found a job to train as a mechanic and was fortunate to work under an excellent foreman who not only really knew his job, but recognised Ray's knowledge gained the hard way by practical experience at the wreckers. From this apprenticeship, Ray progressed and started his own garage and successfully built up his motor business. He saw the potential of Jowetts and was able to secure the distributorship. He provided a full sales and service facility supplemented by having his own workshop, building bodies onto the imported Jowett Bradford chassis.

After Jowett Cars Ltd ceased production, Ray's keen interest did not fade away. It took him along a path which has led him to restore more than a dozen Jowetts up to the present time; he is now in his eighties. Together with Jowett memorabilia, these are housed in a modern building and supplemented by a collection of Speedway 'bikes from his early years, and some other vehicles he has restored. Ray has established a trust for this collection and the Ray Win Museum in Nelson is open by arrangement. It is remarkable that such a collection exists to fly the flag for Jowetts, so far away from the former factory in Idle, Yorkshire. However, Ray still has one really big restoration project that he plans to complete. As many members will know, in 1953 the when the future of the Jowett company was in the balance, plans were in hand to bring out a new model known as the CD.

Much has been written about the prototype and pilot build vehicles and their testing, including the fact that five were exported at the end of 1953 to New Zealand.

CD11 which he acquired several years ago in a substantially dismantled state, really is a major challenge and would be a big job to tackle even for a much younger club member. Many months back, Ray told me of his intentions but unfortunately health reasons were the cause of slow progress. In April he was pleased that an old friend of similar age with much experience who was well enough to come and help. Progress has been slow. In a recent letter Ray told me that 'The CD was the worst condition Jowett that he had done over the years of any Jowetts, and to make matters worse, with it being all pulled apart, we have to do a lot of thinking at times as to where the parts go.' He comments 'I have never had a motor and gearbox so bad to fit back in the chassis, and neither of us want to do another CD! The only good thing about the big body is that it is so versatile and can be used for a delivery van, a station wagon with six seats, or a camper van with two bunks etc.' Ray also likens the rear doors to those of a Standard Vanguard estate car.

Ray and his friend Peter Mckendry have made more progress with the engine now fitted. I hope to be able to bring further updates in the near future. Let's wish them well!

As mentioned previously, this CD was the last Jowett to be restored by Ray Win, who sadly died in May 2012 aged ninety-one. It is now the star exhibit in the Ray Win Museum in Nelson, New Zealand, and is the only restored CD in the world.

I received a letter from Roy Lunn, one of the designers of the CD Bradford range, who told me about how he took one of the CD Estate cars on a proving run to Italy. I forwarded this information to the legendary motoring journalist, Mike Worthington-Williams, who converted it into a very entertaining article for *Classic Car Weekly* newspaper, entitled 'The Italian Job':

If ever a company effectively changed its image irrevocably, without sacrificing its originality and individuality it was Jowett Cars Ltd based in Bradford.

Before the dramatically new streamlined Javelin saloon model burst upon a startled public in 1947, Jowett's reputation had been based on solid ruggedly reliable family cars of agricultural specification and few sporting pretentions. The majority of these had been 7hp flat twins up to 1936 when a flat-four 10hp was introduced.

Post-war, all Jowett cars retained the flat-four engine, but there the similarity to their pre-war ancestors ceased.

The Javelin boasted good lines, independent front suspension and independent rear, both by torsion bars, unitary construction, light weight, superb handling and could do a genuine 80mph, in which combination of features it was unique in Britain at the time.

The space-frame Jupiter two-seater sports from the drawing board of Eberan Von Eberhorst (formerly of Auto Union) was even faster at 90mph.

The pre-war theme was continued on the commercial version, the Bradford van and estate, which retained the horizontally opposed twin-cylinder engine and a separate chassis frame. But by 1951 this design was beginning to show its age, even to commercial users, and plans had been laid for a completely new Bradford model, the CD, which was expected to be in full production by 1953.

In 1949 Gerald Palmer was still chief designer at Jowett and George Wansbrough was chairman, preliminary work had already started on a new all-steel-bodied Bradford.

The project was inherited by the young dynamic Roy Lunn, following Palmer's departure to Morris, and by January 1950 a mock-up had been tested. Mounted on a pressed steel box channel frame, with modified Javelin/Jupiter torsion bar front suspension, the CD was to have leaf springs at the rear, and a body to be made by Briggs, which was also at the time making the Javelin shells. By March 1950 drawings existed for van, estate, pick-up and car versions powered by a new inlet-over-exhaust type flat-twin. The first completed prototype took to the road at the end of 1950 and was registered GKY540.

With experimental body and Javelin front wings, it had covered 14,000 miles by November 1951. In January of the same year, Briggs was told to produce a prototype steel body to drawings supplied, but it was December before it arrived, a hefty six months behind schedule.

Projected tooling costs had also rocketed—from £135,000 to £233,000—which apparently incensed Jowett. They were pleased with the body, which was actually fitted with windows as an estate and registered HKW272.

The CD was designed to take either left or right-hand drive, and subsequently (following an extensive 12-week, 24 hours a day testing period) it was converted to left hand drive.

The purpose of this was enable Lunn, and Ted Fannon of the experimental department, to take the car on a European test run. From the factory at Idle, West Yorkshire, they drove the CD to the south coast, took the ferry to France and travelled via Rheims, Dijon and down to Annecy, there to see Marcel Becquart, with whom Lunn had driven in the RAC Rally. From there they headed towards Lugano, in Switzerland, to pick up another passenger.

He was the son of the owner of Garage del la Ville, the enthusiastic main Jowett agent in the region, had trained at the factory and could speak fluent Italian. He and his brother had amused themselves during their summer holidays by parking a hotted-up Javelin at the foot of the Gothard Pass. They had then chased every Alfa Romeo they saw to the summit. A placard in the rear window proclaimed to the Alfa driver, at the point he was being overtaken that he had just been passed by a 1,500cc Jowett, obtainable from the Garage del la Ville, Lugano! Maybe that's where Jowett coined its slogan, 'Take a good look as it passes you'.

From Lugano, the three adventurers set off into Italy, reaching the coast at the port of Genoa, and then heading south to Pisa.

Roy recalls driving down the coast road, the azure blue Mediterranean on the right, while inland beyond the budding olive trees were snow-capped mountains. He pointed out all of this to Ted, a patriotic Yorkshireman. There was a short pregnant silence whilst Ted digested this remark, and then he said, 'Yorkshire could look like this if it was cleaned up a bit!'

The CD then motored south to Rome, on to Naples and Pompeii before crossing to the Adriatic. They then headed north through Pescara, Ancona and Rimini before crossing the Bologna and back to Lugano,

The trip was most successful proving, as it did, the vehicle's inherent durability and generally showing its capabilities and characteristics.

Nothing untoward occurred throughout, and only normal servicing was carried out, but he does remember driving multi-hairpinned roads with Ted shouting that he wanted danger pay! The return trip across France was accomplished via Lyons, Nevers, Le Mans and Rouen, and then back to Blighty.

Roy left Jowett for Ford in Birmingham, having probably been head-hunted via Briggs (which was taken over by Ford) and thence moved to Dagenham on product planning.

He emigrated to the USA in 1958 to head Ford's advanced engineering department there, being involved in many exciting projects which included the GT40 and Mk 11 and Mark 1V which won Le Mans in 1966, 1967, 1968 and 1969.

In 1971 he joined American Motors as director of Jeep engineering in charge of the Cherokee and CJ-7 projects, and in 1978 he became vice-president of engineering for all AMC and Jeep products.

Sadly, Mike Worthington-Williams died in March 2021 and will be greatly missed by myself and the classic car fraternity as a whole.

To bring things right up to date, Alan Rushworth and I were contacted by the motoring journalist Mike Neale, who was writing an article for the *Classic & Commercial Vehicles* magazine on the CD Bradford range. We both provided information and pictures, and the outcome was a four-page article that appeared in the April 2021 edition with a good selection of pictures. We are hoping this will create more interest in this stillborn range.

Above, below, and next page above: Three views of the CD estate car registered HKW272. (*C. H. Wood*)

Another CD estate car, this one was registered JKW367. (*C. H. Wood*)

Two views of the CD Bradford pick-up. (*C. H. Wood*)

The CD Bradford car. (*C. H. Wood*)

Two views of the part-restored CD estate when owned by Alan Rushworth; his wife, Kathryn, and a young Craig appear with it. This is the only CD Bradford in the UK, which is now owned by another club member who has been working on it for many years. I look forward to seeing it on the road again in the future. (*A. Rushworth*)

Above, below, and opposite page: Four views of the only restored CD estate car, which is on display in the Ray Winn Museum in New Zealand. (*Ray Winn Museum*)

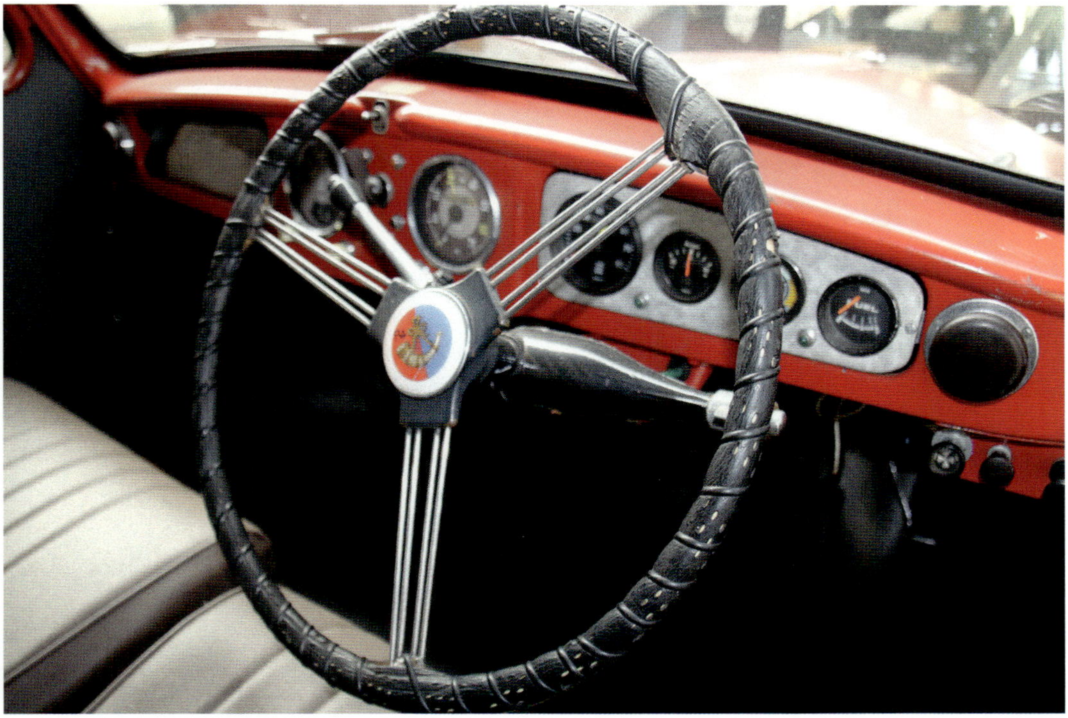

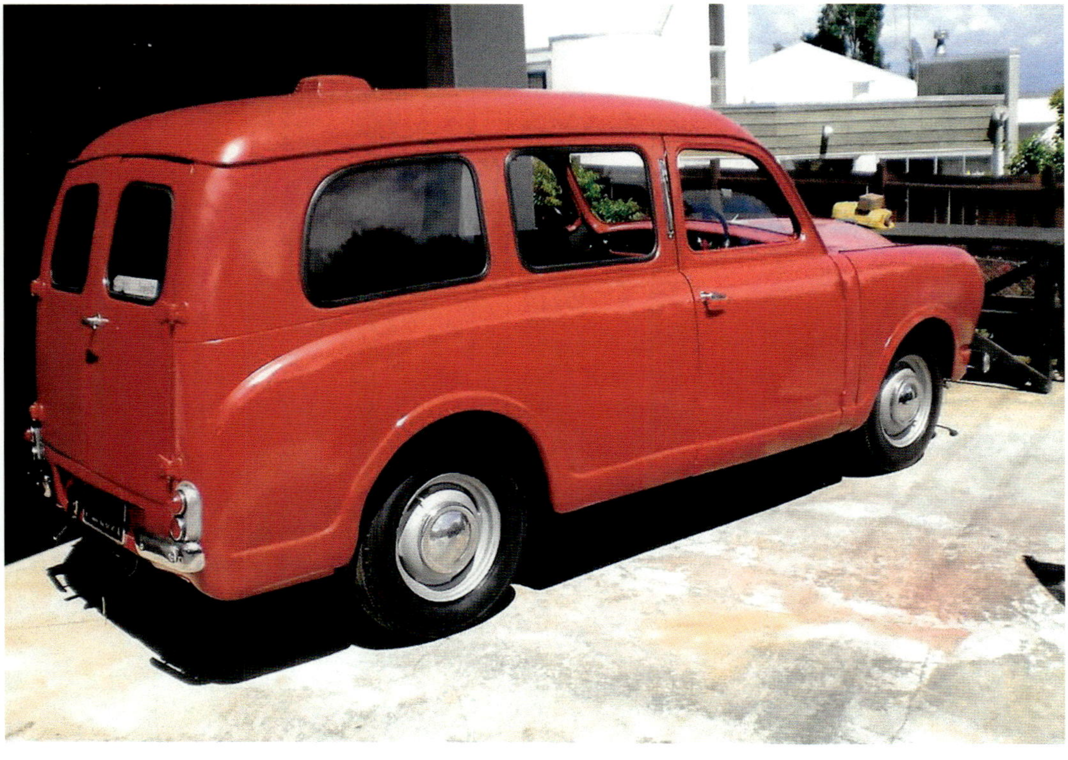

The two other remaining CD estate cars in New Zealand awaiting restoration.

15

1951 AND 1952
R1 JUPITERS

Extract from *The Motor*, 20 June 1951, Listing the 1951 Le Mans Entries

Quite New—In addition to two standard Jupiters, Jowetts will be represented by a prototype similar to the illustration shown and known as the Jupiter R1

Another car that will be running in prototype form is the R1 Jowett Jupiter, a modification of the existing model of this name and is designed purely for the enthusiast who wishes to enter a high-performance production car in sportscar events. It will not, it is understood, be put into large scale production. The engine is similar in design to the production Jupiter, but with the compression ratio increased to 8.5 to 1 giving a maximum power output of 65 bhp at 5,000 rpm giving a bhp figure per square inch of piston area of 2.53 and a piston speed at maximum hp of 2.590 ft/min. Slightly higher gear ratios are employed, top being in the ratio of 4.1 to 1.

In place of the standard Girling Hydro-Mec system brakes are Girling full hydraulic with a mechanically operated hand brake to the rear wheels, and the brake lining has been increased to 122.8 square inches (188 square inches per ton). Fuel is supplied to the engine from a 30-gallon tank from the rear of the car and equipped with two quick-action fillers.

The bodywork of the new model bears but little resemblance to the production Jupiter, being built narrower and lower—the overall height of the car is only 43 inches. The headlamps even though still built-in, are set closer together in the narrow front end which exposes a greater part of the front suspension assembly, and the rocker covers at the head of each set of cylinders.

The reduction of under-bonnet area has obviously resulted in temperature problems which are taken care of by forward facing louvers in each headlamp tunnel and a further set of extractor louvers at the trailing edge of the bonnet.

This car was driven in the 1951 Le Mans twenty-four-hour race by Tommy Wise and Tom Wisdom, the 1950 Le Mans 1.5-litre class winners. It was first registered by Jowett Cars Ltd on 1 June 1951, registered HAK364. Its chassis number was E1/R1/1. The car was incredibly fast and was recorded at 105 mph on the long Mulsanne Straight, but after five hours, it retired with a blown head gasket. This allowed Marcel Becquart and Gordon Wilkins to take the class win for Jowetts for a second time in a standard Jupiter. The times in the standard Jupiter were less impressive than the R1; the best lap average speed in the standard car was 79.633 mph compared to the R1 of 83.373 mph.

This came about because Jowett decided to produce a special competition version of the Jupiter. They said that this would be available to order and it was called the R1. It was hoped that this would make a good competition car and would be produced in small numbers. It was also hoped that successful competition would enhance the slow Jupiter sales. There was a brochure produced, but it is thought by many that this was a smokescreen to deceive the French authorities into thinking this was a production car instead of a one off.

The 'sales brochure' was a single sheet, printed on both sides, which said:

The Jupiter R1 is a competition version of the well-known Jowett Jupiter and has been introduced after a successful career in prototype form to meet the requirements of the owner who wishes to enter sports car races with a high-performance production series in the 1½ litre class. It is eminently suitable for such events as Le Mans, the TT and Production Car Races. This model easily won the 1½ litre race for sports cars at Watkins Glen, USA and competed at Le Mans in 1951.

Tractable under normal road conditions, this model provides outstanding performance, and although of necessity it is small and light, and lacking generous luggage accommodation, the seating provides a high degree of comfort and controllability is excellent.

Based on the Jowett Jupiter Convertible, many of the components are identical. The specification therefore should be read in conjunction with the description of the Jowett Jupiter contained in the catalogue.

Coachwork—The sports body has been designed purely as a lightweight 2-seater for long and short circuit sports car racing. The body is constructed in 20" SWG high tensile light alloy mounted on a light tubular frame rigidly attached to the chassis. It is fitted with racing type fold down aero windscreen and a detachable metal tonneau cover to give a degree of streamline. Two bucket seats are provided of special racing type upholstered in cellular rubber cushioning and special fabric. Limited luggage accommodation is available in the tail. The car is completely equipped with mud wings and full lighting equipment. All electrical equipment is specially mounted on the dashboard for ease of access. It is available in the following colours: British Racing Green or any national colour.

Available extras—special windshield and emergency hood.

Price—These cars are built virtually to special order and a degree of individual requirement can be incorporated.

The R1 was based on a Jupiter chassis and had a light-weight alloy body giving a smaller frontal area, power increased to 70 hp by higher compression ratio at 9.25:1, bigger carburettors, competition distributor, bigger alloy radiator, high-performance Alfin brakes, higher gear ratios, external balance pipe, minimal luggage space, and no roof or windows. It also had cycle-type wings and fairly central headlamps giving it an unusual bug like appearance. Handling was improved by stiffening the bulkhead. It weighed 14 cwt and would reach 100 mph.

In 1952, Jowett produced two more R1s. They also had different front-end bodywork to the original because the Le Mans regulations changed requiring a more enveloping style. The cycle type wings disappeared, and the headlamps were moved further outwards. The appearance of the existing 1951 R1 was altered so that all three 1952 R1 cars had the same appearance. These were chassis number E1/R1/1 registered HAK364, E1/R1/56 registered HKY48, and E1/R1/62 registered HKY49.

Interestingly, Jowett found on testing that the airflow was restricted by the new body style and caused overheating. All the cars had extra cooling openings cut into the front after the cars had left the factory. These three R1s had an unusual light installed on the near side body. These had different colour lenses so at night the pit could identify which car had gone by simply from the colour of this light. These cars were slightly lighter at 13.5 cwt; compression was 9.25:1 and were fitted with Wills Rings and Flexseal gaskets. There were other modifications, all aimed at improving performance and reliability, especially at high rpm. The valves, valve springs, balance pipe, piston rings, pistons, oilways, and con rods all received attention. The crankcase was stiffened with ribbing.

It was incredibly difficult to enter a car from the UK into a foreign race in those days as there was no freedom of movement between European countries. Jowetts had to produce customs documents detailing everything being taken out of the country; this included tools, oil, and spares. This would have run to several pages of detailed information, all of which had to be verified by customs, then cleared on departure and again when returning home. Once at Le Mans, the cars were inspected, after which, no changes were allowed. Apparently, Jowett then found that they needed to change a jet in the carburettors as the cars were not running well, but this was not allowed. Rumour has it that the Zenith carburettor engineer brought new jets into the Jowett pit with them hidden in his mouth.

Only one of the three R1 cars finished but came first in the 1.5-litre class by virtue of the fact it was the only car still running. By this time though, the competition in the class had increased dramatically. Porsche had entered a car for the first time and were much faster than the R1. Luckily for Jowetts, it was disqualified for not turning its engine off when calling into the pits during the race. A little less known is that another Porsche won the 1.1-litre class in a faster time than the R1. The Jowett board realised that their engine was being outclassed as it was never designed for racing. A new engine design was out of the question as by this time, the Jowett Company was struggling due to slow sales of both the Javelin and Jupiter.

The rest of the R1 story is perhaps not as well known, as Jowetts chopped up the R1 cars and put them on their scrap heap, as at that time, it was usual for manufacturers of racing cars to keep them. It was said that if they were sold, they would have had to pay purchase tax on them and would also have to supply spares for years to come. The cars were broken-up to avoid this situation. The chassis were cut in half to prevent them from being used again in the future.

Fortunately, this is not the end of the story as one car has been reassembled like a phoenix rising from the ashes—or should I say spares? This came about as a Jowett employee, Eric Price, bought two halves of one chassis plus the original Alfin brakes and other parts for the princely sum of £30. He was able to put it back as a running car, but not to the original specification; it even had a Vauxhall engine fitted as he could not afford a Jowett one.

It was then purchased by Roger Barrett, who ran it for a while. I was lucky enough to see it in this form at the Jowett Car Club rally in York in 1974. After this, it was loaned to the Bradford Industrial Museum for display for a few years until he sold it to Dennis Sparrow and Peter Dixon in 1978. They moved it from Bradford to Dennis's workshop in West London, and the Vauxhall engine was replaced by a Javelin engine. The car still had many incorrect parts, so this was the start of an eighteen-year restoration to bring the car back to its original 1952 Le Mans specification. They made a fantastic job of this as every detail is correct. It has since taken part in various historic races, including Le Mans twice, Goodwood Revival, and Monaco. It was also the subject of a lengthy article in the March 2019 issue of *Octane* magazine, with some stunning pictures of it.

The car is currently for sale through Arun Holdings of Bordon Hampshire and is described as follows:

The ex-works Jowett Jupiter R1, the sole surviving one of three works racing cars. This is a unique piece of English Le Mans history, winning its class at Le Mans in 1952, driven by Marcel Becquart and Gordon Wilkins. The car was found in Bradford, where the original factory was and has been restored over the years to original specification using original chassis and bodywork. It has full FIA papers, lots of history including many pictures of the car in period, and of its rebuild. The car has taken part in many races including The Goodwood Revival, two Le Mans Legends and would be eligible for Monaco, having raced in a sports car race there in period.

For sale now after being in the same ownership for the last 40 years and at a very reasonable price….

As of February 2022, the car is still for sale; it can be yours for £199,999.

The R1 JUPITER *a new prototype model which made its debut at Le Mans in 1951 and is at present being developed for competition work. The R1 is a lighter version of the Jupiter, giving more b.h.p. and higher speed.*

Major Javelin and Jupiter successes

1949

JAVELIN 1949 Monte Carlo Rally, 1½-litre Class
1st T. C. Wise
3rd R. Smith

JAVELIN Austrian Touring Club Winter Trial, 2-litre Class
1st Herr Wohrer

JAVELIN Rheineck/Walzenhausen Hill Climb
1½-litre Class, Touring
1st Herr Vogelsang

JAVELIN 24-hour Belgian Grand Prix, Spa
2-litre Touring Class
1st A. Hume and T. H. Wisdom. 65·5 m.p.h.

1950

JAVELIN Rallye des Neiges, general classification
1st Herr Gurzeler.

JUPITER Le Mans 24-hour Grand Prix d'Endurance
1½-litre Class
1st T. H. Wisdom and T. C. Wise. Course record for class. The only Jupiter running in its first race. 75·8 m.p.h.

JAVELIN Vues des Alpes Hill Climb
1½-litre Class, Experts
1st Herr Vogelsang

1951

JUPITER and **JAVELIN** Monte Carlo Rally, 1½-litre Class
1st W. H. Robinson and R. Ellison—Jupiter*†
2nd G. Wilkins and R. F. Baxter—Jupiter†
4th L. Odell and R. Marshall—Javelin†
* Best English competitor (shared) and 6th in general classification
† Manufacturer's team prize

JAVELIN Swedish Winter Trial
1st Sven Servais

JUPITER Lisbon Rally, general classification
1st Joachim Noqueria

JUPITER Bremgarten Sports Car Race, 1½-litre Class
1st Herr Gurzeler

JUPITER Rheineck/Walzenhausen Hill Climb, 1½-litre Class
1st Herr Gurzeler

JUPITER Le Mans 24-hour Grand Prix d'Endurance
1½-litre Class
1st M. Becquart and G. Wilkins. 71·9 m.p.h. (only car in class to finish)

JUPITER R.A.C Tourist Trophy Race, 1½-litre Class
1st H. L. Hadley
2nd T. C. Wise

JUPITER Watkins Glen Meeting, 1½-litre race
1st George Weaver

A page from the *50 Years of Progress* booklet by Jowett Cars Ltd featuring the 1951 R1 Jupiter.

The JOWETT JUPITER. R.1.

THE JUPITER R.1. is a competition version of the well-known JOWETT JUPITER, and has been introduced after a successful career in prototype form to meet the requirements of the owner who wishes to enter sports car races with a high performance production series car in the 1½ litre class. It is eminently suitable for such events as Le Mans, the T.T. and Production Car Races. This model easily won the 1½ litre race for Sports Cars at Watkins Glen, U.S.A., and competed at Le Mans in 1951.

Tractable under normal road conditions, this model provides outstanding performance, and although of necessity it is small and light, and lacking generous luggage accommodation, the seating provides a high degree of comfort and controllability is excellent.

Based on the JOWETT JUPITER Convertible, many of the components are identical. The specification should therefore be read in conjunction with the description of the JOWETT JUPITER contained in the catalogue. Points of difference are noted below and overleaf.

TECHNICAL SPECIFICATION

Engine

Compression Ratio	9·25 : 1.
Power output	Maximum power 70 b.h.p. at 5,000 r.p.m.
Camshaft	High lift with increased overlap.
Carburettor	Twin Zenith of special type.

Chassis

Frame	Basically same as Jupiter.
Brake Drums	Al-Fin composite aluminium and cast iron construction 9" diameter on brake track by 1¾" wide.
Brake Lining Area	122·8 sq. in., equivalent to 188 sq. in. per ton.

Dimensions

Overall Length 160".	Approx. dry weight 12 cwt.
Overall Width 58".	Ground clearance 7".
Height 43".	Petrol tank 30 gallons.

Transmission and Performance

Ratios—Top 4·1 : 1.			
3rd 5·63 : 1.	Synchro-	1st 14·62 : 1.	
2nd 8·91 : 1.	mesh.	Rev. 14·62 : 1.	

Top gear per 1,000 r.p.m.—19·4 m.ph.
Top gear at 2,500 ft./min. piston speed 82 m.p.h.

Instruments

A 5" specially calibrated revolution indicator and speedometer, engine oil pressure and temperature gauge, radiator thermometer, ammeter and fuel indicator.

Above and below: Both sides of a single-sheet sales brochure. Some think that this was a ploy to encourage the scrutineers at Le Mans to think that this was in fact a production model.

1½ litre JOWETT JUPITER. R.1. contd.

Coachwork

The sports body has been designed purely as a light weight 2-seater for long and short circuit sports car racing. The body is constructed of 20" SWG high tensile light alloy mounted on a light tubular frame rigidly attached to the chassis. It is fitted with racing type fold flat aero windscreen and a detachable metal tonneau cover to give a high degree of streamline. Two bucket seats are provided of special racing type upholstered in cellular rubber cushioning and special fabric. Limited luggage accommodation is available in the tail. The car is completely equipped with mudwings and full road lighting equipment. All electrical equipment is specially mounted on the dashboard for ease of access. It is available in the following colours: British Racing Green or any national colour to order.

Available extras—Special windshield and emergency hood.

Price—These cars are built virtually to special order and a degree of individual requirement can be incorporated.

JOWETT CARS LTD., IDLE, BRADFORD, YORKS., and 48 ALBEMARLE STREET, W.1

The 1951 R1 Jupiter in its original form with motorcycle-type front wings ready for the 1951 Le Mans twenty-four-hour race. (*C. H. Wood*)

The 1952 R1 Jupiter with the built-in front wings to comply with the amended regulations for the 1952 Le Mans twenty-four-hour race. (*C. H. Wood*)

Left: The winning R1 Jupiter at the finish of the 1952 Le Mans twenty-four-hour race with Marcel Becquart in the driver's seat; Gordon Wilkins, the motoring journalist, was the co-driver in the passenger seat. The average speed was 72.85 mph. (*Louis Klemantaski*)

Below: Another view of the winning car, *left to right*: Gordon Wilkins, Charles Grandfield, Arthur Jopling, and Marcel Becquart. (*JCC Archive*)

The engine bay of the 1952 R1. (*C. H. Wood*)

The surviving R1 at the Jowett Car Club rally in 2005 in Basingstoke.

Another view of the R1, this time at the Jowett Car Club Rally in 2010 in Wakefield.

The R1 at speed. (*Octane magazine*)

The R1 at night. (*Octane magazine*)

Two views of the R1 whilst the car was for sale in early 2021 by Arun Holdings at the stunning price of £199,000. The car remained unsold at the time of writing (June 2021). (*Arun Holdings*)

16

1952
Mᴋ 2 Jᴜᴘɪᴛᴇʀ

Iɴ ᴛʜᴇ ᴀʀᴄʜɪᴠᴇ of C. H. Wood (Bradford) Ltd (Jowett's official photographer), there were some photographs from 1952 showing the 'plasticine' model and paper factory drawings for a Mk 2 Jupiter with various sketches of how the car would look. These were drawn by Phil Stephenson showing the Mk 2 body design, which was based on the standard and well-proven Jupiter chassis, with some modification to the very rear section. It was planned that this would be the next-generation Jupiter, but sadly, due to the limited resources at Jowett, these were diverted to the development of the R4, so the Mk 2 was shelved.

In 2008, Alan Fishburn, an accomplished panel maker who had worked on the restoration of several standard-bodied Jupiters, read about the Mk 2 Jupiter and became very keen to recreate the car using the factory drawings. A Mk 1a Jupiter chassis E3/SC/944R, registered 2258E, was located, the body of which had been badly damaged in a collision with a bus in 1961. Alan set to work building the body in aluminium, and by slightly modifying the near side chassis member, he was able to move the engine mounting backwards by 2 inches, which allowed the radiator to be mounted in front of the engine. By using an adapted VW Golf water pump, it lowered the overall engine height to fit within the dimensions of the factory drawings. In 2010, Alan was able to trailer the almost completed Mk 2 to the Jowett Car Club Centenary Rally at Wakefield. I was there and can confirm it created a great deal of interest.

In December 2011, the Mk 2 was a running car and passed its MOT. In September 2012, it was displayed at the Croft circuit, which, once again, created a lot of interest. In 2013, Alan decided to give up his business and sell the Mk 2 Jupiter. It changed hands in 2015 with Alan retaining the 2258E registration; the Mk2 is now carrying its new registration number, 733UYL.

Steve Collier was the new owner and recognising the significance of this Jupiter, he began a programme of work to refine it. A tremendous amount of work has been carried out on the car and has now been completed to a very high standard, including a respray in metallic green; it has also been retrimmed.

Technically, this car is not a special but more of a faithful interpretation of what the manufacturer had intended had circumstances been different.

In November 2017, the car graced the Jowett Car Club stand of the Lancaster insurance Classic Motor Show at the NEC, where it was reported:

Although still work in progress, the car attracted a huge amount of attention with comments such as 'it looks similar to an AC Ace from the front' and even a member of the Ferrari Tifosi thought it had the look of a 166 of the early 1950s. Oh praise indeed.

Jupiter Owners' Auto Club—By *Jupiter Magazine* No. 1 2018

The car was advertised for sale on the *Car & Classic* website in February 2021 (which they referred to as a R2 Jupiter, rather than its correct title of a Mark 2 Jupiter), as follows:

JOWETT SPECIAL BODIED R2 1953 For Sale

This 1953 JOWETT R2 is the only one in existence, The Jupiter Mk2 was designed by Jowett in 1952 as a competitor to the TR2 but never built. In 2008, respected Jowett restorer, Allan Fishburn, created a one-off Mk 2 (from the original drawings) based on a 1953 Jowett Jupiter chassis and rebuilt engine, clothed in hand-beaten aluminium panels Recently restored by TW Brotherton in Blockley. This involved stripping most of the panels replacing all internal boot and engine bay panels and full inside and out respray. Cost of work circa £12,000 The car has new instruments and brand-new tailored wiring loom. The car has matching numbers, 733UYL is a work in progress and requires some finishing. When complete, this superbly finished, delightful little fifties' sports car will be a work of art, Unique and important. Your opportunity to complete a chapter in Jowett's history.

REGISTRATION: 733 UYL Right Hand Drive.

YEAR: 1953 ENGINE SIZE: 1.5 litres.

Chassis number: E3/SC/944R

Head gasket needs replacing, and braking system needs overhauling, it also needs a new petrol tank and door latches 3. The car is almost there and is a unique opportunity to acquire a one off.

The asking price was a very optimistic £49,000. The car did not sell at that time.

The car was advertised by Silverstone Auctions of Ashorne, Warwickshire, in their auction of 22 May 2021; the following is part of the description of the car:

Over £50,000 invested in this fascinating story of 'what might have been'. Jowett's sporty Mk2 Jupiter brought to life.

Fully designed and ready to go to the next stage, plans for the second-generation of Jowett's successful Jupiter were shelved when the company closed in 1954.

The drawings and plans for the aborted 'Mk 2' were discovered in 1979 and subsequently acquired by Jowett enthusiast and restorer Allan Fishburn. A man of vision, he began building a one-off Jupiter Mk2 using the chassis and engine of a damaged Mk1A Jupiter. Completed around 2011 but not used, it was purchased in 2016 by our vendor who also shared the vision of bringing a Jupiter Mk 2 to life.

The all-aluminium body was stripped and restored in early 2017 by TW Brotherton of Blockley. New engine bay and boot panels, realigning all panels and a bare metal respray. (296 hours—£12,000+)

Further work by MB Restorations in Bradford included an engine and gearbox rebuild, new aluminium petrol tank, custom radiator and grille, exhaust and brakes.

Finally, a £2,800.00 full quality leather retrim was undertaken along with a new tonneau cover.

Now superbly presented in 'Verde Isola' with a smart cabin trimmed in Olive Green quilted leather.

Fabulous attention to detail throughout. Smiths white-faced instruments, Jowett wood-rim wheel, Lucas headlights, split-screen, twin exhausts and Pirelli Cinturatos.

Fascinating history file with photographs of the restoration and the car on the Jowett Car Club stand at the NEC, a copy of a photo of the Mk 2 clay model, copies of various technical drawings and invoices totalling £28,652 (£15,000 from 2019/20 alone).

The description of the car concludes with:

Different and quirky it may be, but Jowetts were always different and quirky, and this good-looking little roadster encompasses everything you might hope to find in a fifties' sports car. This is a unique opportunity to own and drive the physical incarnation of the dreams and aspirations of those enthusiastic young draughtsmen who toiled away in the Jowett drawing office some seven decades ago and close the final chapter in the story of the Jowett Car Company.

Surprisingly, the car only managed to sell for £21,938 (which includes the buyer's premium), so I think the new owner got a real bargain.

Sketches of the proposed Mk 2 Jupiter.

A plasticine model of the Mk 2 Jupiter, which was an abandoned project and progressed no further. (*C. H. Wood*)

Above, below, and next page: Three views of the Mk 2 creation, built by Alan Fishburn, pictured at Croft racetrack in 2014.

Opposite page: Two views of the Mk 2 at the NEC Classic Car Show in 2017. It was nearing completion of a full rebuild by the new owner of the car.

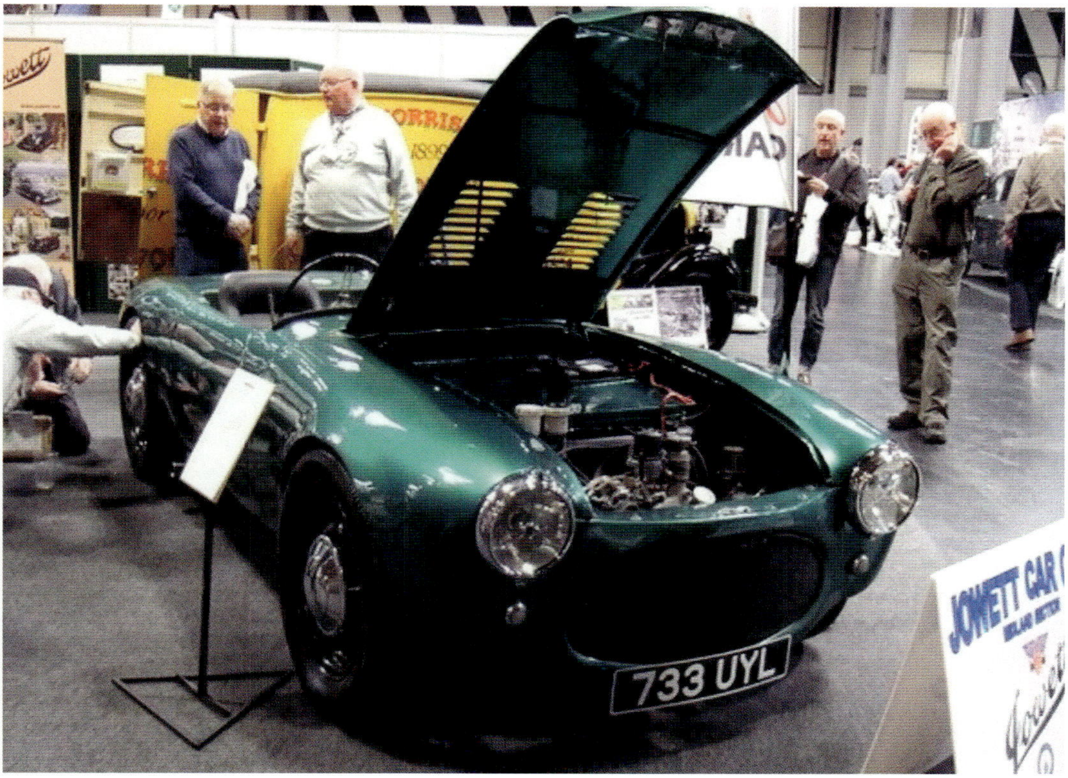
733 UYL
JOWETT CAR C

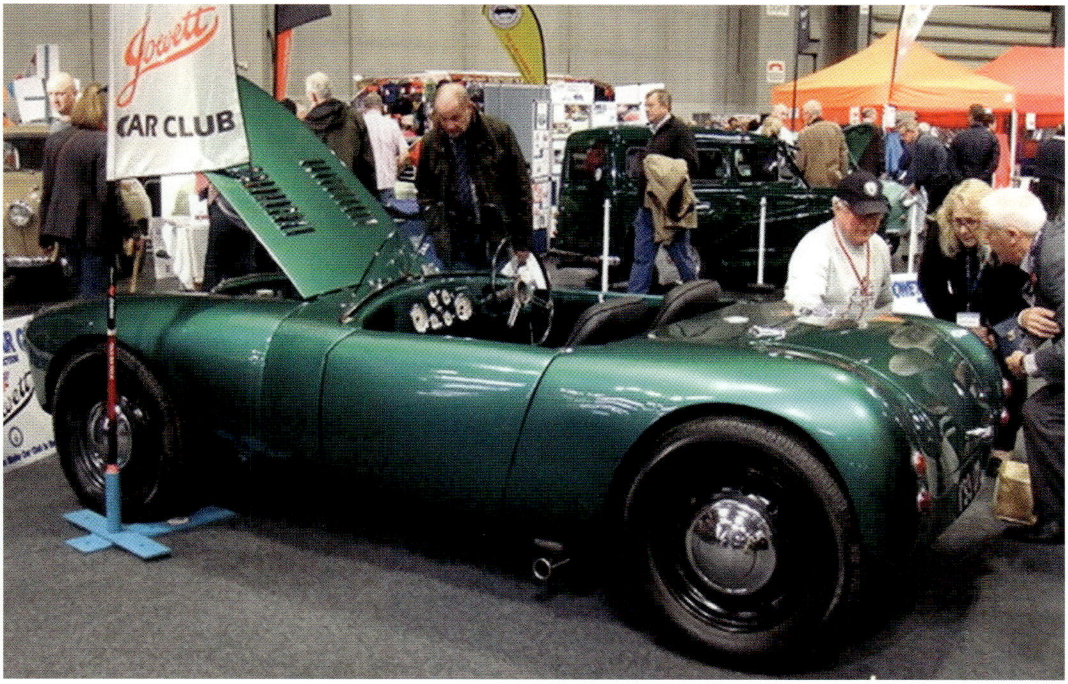
Jowett
CAR CLUB

Two views of the completed Mk 2 Jupiter when it was being advertised for sale with Silverstone Auctions in May 2021; sadly, it did not reach the price the seller was hoping for by a large margin. (*Silverdale Auctions*)

17

1953
Jupiter R4

THE R4 JUPITER was Jowett's last-ditch effort at car manufacture. By mid-1953, the supply of Javelin bodies had ceased from Briggs, so if any kind of car production was to continue, it would have to be without any involvement from them. It was suggested that if a car could be ready to have on display on the stand for the Earls Court Motor Show in October, it could possibly save the company. This was an ambitious plan, as it only gave the Experimental Department just over three months to do this. They started experiments with fibreglass laminate and resin plastic in the hope that they could build a car in-house, which would have meant that a pressed steel facility would not have been needed. The original styling of the car was carried out by Phil Stephenson, who also styled the stillborn Mk 2 Jupiter detailed previously. Both these cars had a very similar design, but differed considerably, as the R4 was much shorter, using the modified shortened chassis from the CD Bradford range, whereas the Mk 2 was designed round the original, much longer, Jupiter chassis. The original name for the car was the Jupiter 100, as it was expected to be able to top 100 mph, but was later advertised as the Jupiter R4.

The project was headed up by Donald Bastow, who was recruited by Jowetts in September 1952. He had previously worked for Rolls-Royce and Lagonda. He was a very talented engineer, and prior to starting on the R4, he resolved various technical problems, including Javelin/Jupiter oil cooling and a stronger crankshaft. The team also included Roy Lunn, who replaced Gerald Palmer (the Javelin designer), who returned to the Nuffield Group in 1949, and Phil Stephenson, both of whom did a considerable amount of detail work on the CD and R4.

The Experimental Department worked all hours that God sent on the project and were rewarded with having the first prototype completed in the summer of 1953. This was steel-bodied, but the following two R4 production prototypes were part-steel and part-fibreglass. One of these was ready for the Earls Court Show (just) and was very well received by the motoring press, including a full road test in *The Motor* of 21 October 1953. This road test follows, plus a couple of first-hand accounts of how this car was produced and shows how it was finished by the skin of their teeth.

Jowett Jupiter R4, *The Motor* 21 October 1953, also in *The Motor* Yearbook 1954

In the past 12 months competition in sports-car racing has become so keen that success can only be achieved by cars designed to give speeds and acceleration considerably higher than have been thought *adequate in past seasons.*

The Jowett Co. have responded to this situation by the introduction of the R4 Jupiter, the overall design of which differs materially from the type Mark IA although the power units employed are very similar. Taking advantage of the high-octane values of currently obtainable premium fuels, the R4 engine has been given a compression ratio of 8.5:1 which has raised the output on the track to 65hp. at 5,000rpm This corresponds to a piston speed of just under 3,000 ft./min. and the peak of the torque curve lies between 2,750 and 3,000rpm., that is to say, between 45 and 50 m.p.h. on the normal final axle ratio.

As with all other post-war Jowett models, the four cylinders in two opposed pairs are placed well forward of the front wheel centre line, the four-speed gearbox lying beneath the radiator core which is placed on the wheel centre line. A unique feature of the R4 Jupiter is an electrically driven fan placed just behind the core and linked to a thermostat. This electric fan drive gives the designer a good deal more freedom than normal in the relative position of the radiator and the engine and eliminates the need for driving the fan from the engine itself. There is almost no weight penalty as the weight of the electric motor is offset by the use of a smaller and lighter radiator. This in turn follows from the fact that in traffic conditions where the fan would normally be turning at low speed with the engine idling the fan comes in and runs at a high speed until the water temperature is reduced to normal. A similar situation arises when climbing hills at low speeds (as when following other traffic) and when a first or even second gear is not needed by the steepness of the gradient.

In ordinary running on the road the air flow through the radiator is such as to keep the water temperature at the required level without the use of the fan so that those who are doubtful of the reliability of all electrical contrivances will be comforted by knowing that breakdown will not affect the normal operation of the car.

Although the electrically driven fan is undoubtedly the most technically interesting of the changes made, the new frame design is also of particular interest. The previous tubular structure has been replaced by box-section pressings of quite exceptional depth. The chassis is further reinforced by welded-on steel scuttle, but a large proportion of the body panels are made of resin-impregnated glass fibre. This new material has remarkable qualities which are referred to in detail in the chapter dealing with technical developments. It will therefore suffice to say that the use of the material on the R.4 in conjunction with smaller dimensions and the new frame has resulted in the exceptionally low weight of 14 cwt. dry, 25 per cent. less than the Mark IA model, although the overall stiffness of the structure is appreciably improved.

There are three more major differences between the two cars. At the front the rack and pinion steering gear hitherto used is replaced by a Bishop cam and lever, this being one of the very few instances where a manufacturer has ever discarded the rack and pinion type. A second, at the back, is the replacement of torsion bars and trailing arm plus Panhard rod for suspension and axle control, by the more conventional semi-elliptic leaf springs. A third, placed mid-way in the car, is an overdrive gear which is mounted between two cross members and thus divides the propeller shaft into two sections. The ratio of this component is such as to reduce the engine speed by 18 per cent. and the effect on overall performance may be considered by taking the speeds reached on the read at the peak of the hp curve. On the three upper ratios of the conventional gearbox these are 35, 56, and 83.5 m.p.h. Using overdrive third as well as overdrive top we get 35, 56, 68, 83.5, and

102 m.p.h. The actual top speed realized on the road will depend in part on the condition in which the car is run, since the frontal area of 16½ sq. ft. with a full screen is reduced to 13.6 sq. ft. with one aero screen, as would be used for competition purposes. A true maximum of over 100mph can, however, be confidently anticipated.

The car was well profiled despite the remarkably short wheelbase of only 7 feet. It is interesting to observe that the car is pronouncedly crab-tracked, a practice in competition cars which dates back to the 1927 Grand Prix Sunbeams. The fact that the model is avowedly designed for competition has not been allowed to stand in the way of high standards of finish and equipment. These can be well judged from the illustrations and from inspection of the Earls Court in the next ten days.

This last paragraph is how the article finished in *The Motor* London Motor Show issue of 21 October 1953. The same article also appeared in *The Motor Yearbook of 1954*, except for the last paragraph, which was substituted for the one below:

Although, as first announced, this model (despite its exceptionally low price) appealed primarily to the competition driver, the constructors were actively engaged in the development of a closed version, one form of which is a quickly detachable top. It may therefore confidently be expected that the R4 will obtain a considerable fraction of the sales in the market for small sports cars.

The R4 Jupiter had another mention in *The Motor of* 21 October 1953, which referred to the car as 'Bradford's Thunderbolt' and went on to say:

The R4 Jupiter with 65bhp from a 1½-litre engine the engine the attention of the designer has been devoted primarily to reducing weight and wind resistance. He has in consequence made a very small car with a 7-foot wheelbase and a frontal area of only 16½ square feet even with a full screen in position. Once again, we see the inclusion of an overdrive in the specification, this unit being placed in the propeller-shaft line. The frame has deep steel box sections welded to the body panels so as to form a very stiff assembly.

Ernest Horsfall, who worked in the Experimental Department, described the project as follows:

The rush was on to produce a car to be displayed at the London Motor Show held in October 1953. With only a few months to go some staff involved on the R4 worked long hours to get the car ready. I frequently worked two days without a stop then, with just a few hours' sleep, worked on for another day. For me and others, this continued until just before the show. The effort was tremendous, but the target was achieved: an R4 for London.

Having worked until late on the Friday before the Motor Show, I was in bed on the Saturday morning when at around 10 o'clock, the Experimental Department Supervisor called at our house. Still in my pyjamas, I went downstairs, and he said that he had come to ask me to drive the Bedford Truck and take the R4 to the show venue at Earls Court, London. He had arranged for Harry, one of the fitters, to go with me. Now Harry, apart from working at Jowetts, was a drummer in a local band and was to play that Saturday evening. The result was quite hilarious for I had to collect him at the dance. We could not set off until they'd played the last waltz, after which Harry climbed into the cab in his evening dress, and I took him home to change. As a passenger, I guess he thought he would be able to nod off, but this was not to be. Due to some areas of thick fog he had to walk in front of the lorry on occasions until we got to Wakefield.

Having lost time, I put my foot down where I could. As an unfortunate consequence, we had a brush with the law in the early hours when a police car pulled us over going through Newark at 50 mph. I apologised to the officer who remarkably accepted our explanation that Harry had played in a band, we had been delayed by fog, and the car on the back was a Jowett which had to be delivered to the London Motor Show by morning. He smiled and said, "Good luck with the Jowett and take care. Follow me and I'll lead you through the town". We breathed a sigh of relief and pressed on! On arrival at Earls Court, our problems were not over, for we found that the brakes on the R4 had locked up. With a struggle and many helpers, eventually the R4 was lifted off the truck. With brakes freed, it was then pushed onto the Jowett stand. Company staff made final adjustments to its position where the standing appearance of the car was improved by filling the fuel tank with sand. However further trouble was waiting to happen. During the show the heat from the lights over the stand began to take its toll on the car's fibre glass and finish. Rectification took place during the night hours. Despite the commitment of the hard-working staff, and at £545 before tax the R4 being the cheapest 100mph car at the show, only prototypes were produced. By the end of the year, with continuing difficulties at the company, Roy Lunn left to join Ford, and International Harvester were negotiating to buy the factory at Idle.

At the time of sending this manuscript to my publishers in February 2022, Ernest is still going strong at the incredible age of 103, with a memory that is second to none.

Phill Green, who also worked in the Experimental Department at Jowetts, remembered these events:

It was in June 1953 that Charles Grandfield gathered together all the Experimental staff when he addressed them, ending with the words 'Jowett's are on their way out!' But then he threw the lifeline about getting a car to Earls Court in three months.

We already had Roy Lunn's drawings of the basic R4—not by name, but as a sporting two-seater, and so work was immediately started on the initial steel-bodied R4 which Roy Lunn and Teddy Fannon were to take down through Italy on a proving run. The chassis was CD-based because the dimensions were just about right; the engine was 'breathed upon' to get more performance, and the shaft-driven radiator cooler was removed from the water pump and an electric fan installed behind the radiator: this measure saved 4bhp. The two seats were steel pans which we filled with plaster of Paris and then I sat in them wearing clean overalls, and when they set, we took the block of plaster to Dunlopillo at Pannal outside Harrogate and asked them to cast the blocks in Dunlopillo latex—beautiful!

The four-speed gearbox was based on the tested CD gearbox, to which was attached a Laycock de Normanville overdrive unit; forward view was protected by a pair of glass aero screens. Of course, we then had to set about making two glassfibre bodies, since we had no more allocated steel. Fibreglass chemists from Gravesend were employed to create the bodies in the style of the original steel bodied R4. And so, by an absolutely amazing effort by the whole of Experimental Department, during which engineers built metal parts and drawing office staff followed them around drawing the newly fabricated components, we built three R4s in time for the 1953 Show! September's issue of *Glass's Guide* published advanced notice of the R4 priced at £773, all in! A white R4 was the principal exhibit on the Jowett stand; we had a pale grey and maroon R4 in our London Albemarle Street showroom, and I had the original steel-bodied car to demonstrate to prospective customers around London.

I have never seen a team of men work like it, before or since! It was one of the most amazing operations that I have ever been a part of, and I shall NEVER forget it!

The all-steel prototype was sold to Alf Thomas, a garage proprietor in Bedford; he later acquired the other two. He entered all three cars in Silverstone's six-hour race on 16 August 1958, which raced as a team. Sadly, two of the cars were damaged in the race, so Alf retired from racing. These two cars were repaired and in 1960 he sold all three to Peter Michael, who apparently sold his mother's car to raise the £1,500 to pay for them. By the early 1960s, all three had been sold, and all had been involved in heavy crashes, one terminally. The remaining two, the all-steel car registered JKW547 and the show car SWT356, were both restored and have had various owners since then. In 1985, SWT356 was owned by Ian Pritchett, who once again entered the car in sporting events. He also made the car available to the *Classic & Sportscar* magazine, who road tested it for the March 1986 issue. I personally would not have called the car 'The Ugly Duckling', but it was an interesting article nonetheless:

'The Ugly Duckling' by Mark Gillies, *Classic & Sportscar*, March 1986

Just before Jowett ceased production, the company made a last-ditch effort to produce a modern new sports car. Mark Gillies wonders if the R4 could have saved the firm.

Jowett's R4 Jupiter has to be a contender for the motoring Ugly Bug Ball. It looks as though it was styled by three different people: the cheeky grille which overhangs too far, the bizarre front wings and the peculiar wasp waisting of the sills mark this out as a great styling disaster. It may appear to be aping Touring's masterly Ferrari Barchetta body, but there's no contest.

However, you have to regard the car in its true context. First, it was a last-ditch attempt by a firm very much in its death throes. And second, it was a startling new shape in an era of stuffy conservatism from the British motor industry. Several features, such as leather trimmed cockpit surround and the hooded instruments, were more American than British, with slight Corvette overtones.

The car really forms an epitaph for the illustrious Jowett concern, which was scuppered by circumstances beyond its control. The takeover of Briggs, the body building firm, by Ford in 1953 meant that Jowetts had no means of making bodies for its Bradford vans and Javelin saloons. Nobody else would step in, and Jowett could not fill the gap either.

The Jowett Experimental Department was, however, asked to produce a new sportscar on the basis that this would be the only way of saving the company. It needed to be cheap, easy to make and not involve any work by Briggs.

Time was short and the car had to be ready for the Earls Court Motor Show in October 1953. As the engine and running gear was from the existing Jupiter sports car, with the proven flat-four 1486cc pushrod overhead valve unit under the bonnet. It ran a higher compression ratio (8.5:1) and a different camshaft profile to increase the power output from 62.5bhp at 4,500rpm to 64bhp at 5,000rpm.

The engine was mated to a four-speed gearbox with wide ratio Javelin gear clusters. The 4.44:1 final drive ratio gave a theoretical top speed of 102–105mph with the optional overdrive fitted.

There was a live rear axle, sprung by torsion bars and Panhard rod, while the independent front suspension was by wishbones with transverse link, again with the torsion bar springing, Where the car truly differed from its predecessor was in its chassis and chosen of construction.

Instead of the ordinary Jupiter's tubular frame, there was a fabricated box section affair, reinforced by a welded-on scuttle and tail panel—it was both lighter and stiffer than the conventional Jupiter. Designer Roy Lunn—later to work for Ford—decided that the only way to get around the problem with body supply was to experiment with fibre reinforced plastic. Despite numerous problems with this material, two pre-production cars had FRP front bodywork sections. The first R4, registered JKW547, was all metal and was finished in July 1953, just five months after the project had been initialled.

At the Motor Show, one of the other two cars was on the firm's stand and was to be later registered SWT356. It was the cheapest car capable of 100mph at the show, priced at just £777 4s 2d.

The appearance at Earls Court and later at the Scottish Motor Show in November were the last acts of the firm. December saw International Harvester and the Blackburn & General Aircraft Co move in to take over Jowett. But that was not the end of the R4 story, due mainly to the efforts of Jowett enthusiast and Bedfordshire garage proprietor, Alf Thomas. He bought the prototype in 1954, purchasing the show car and third R4, unsold when Jowett went under. In 1958 all three appeared in a team for the Silverstone Six Hours Relay Race. The R4 proved quite a competitive club sports car, JKW537 regularly lapping faster than MGA's and TR2's around Silverstone.

Thomas sold all three cars in 1960, and they all suffered accidents subsequently. The third car was totalled, but the other two survived. The show car was bought by Arthur Rutland in 1967, who restored it over a period of 12 years. When he died it went to his son Len Jones and thence to current owner Ian Pritchett. The prototype car is currently undergoing restoration.

To find out whether there's a supercar trying to escape from that plug ugly exterior, Ian kindly let me drive the car. First impressions are a little confusing. The outlook is dominated by the short dumpy bonnet, while you sit well forward and relatively high up in the comfortable bucket seats. Looking at the instrument panel with its array of white-faced dials, unique to these cars (there were only three such sets made) you could be sitting in a later car but for the huge steering wheel relatively close to the driver's chest.

Pedal positioning is well thought out, and the gear lever, a smooth metal topped device, falls perfectly to hand. Other deft touches include the roller type throttle pedal, and the dashboard mounted overdrive switch and a horn lever which operates whichever way you tilt it.

The car's engine makes a lovely boxer growl, similar to an Alfasud, and has plenty of torque on tap. It certainly has enough power there to justify claims of a sub-13 seconds 0–60mph time when new. The gear change is almost instant with a lovely combination of precision and speed. The cam and lever steering are responsive and positive, while the underlying handling balance is pleasantly neutral, even if the car's short wheelbase makes one wary of pushing it. Ian has taken part in the Coronation Rally in the car and found the on-the-limit handling reassuring, especially considering the fact that all three cars had been badly crashed at one time.

One over-riding impression, though, is of how relaxed the car is, especially for a fifties 1½-litre sports car. With overdrive engaged, 70mph equates to just over 3,000rpm, while the ride tends to cosset you extremely well from bumps. It is all so much more civilised than contemporary MG's and TR's, which seem to regard ride quality as caught in a time warp—somewhere in the thirties.

Yes, there is a super little car trying to escape from under that exterior. It has to be one of the true nearly cars. If only Jowett had had the time and money to develop it properly, it would surely have been a winner.

It is amazing to think that two of the three R4s built still survive, considering all three had been involved in heavy crashes in the 1960s. It is testament to club members, who, over the years, have restored these cars, bringing them back to life.

An original sketch of the proposed R4 Jupiter by Phill Stephenson; note: it was originally going to be called the Jupiter 100 as it was capable of reaching 100 mph. (*Thoroughbred & Classic Car magazine*)

The old and the new—the original Jupiter at the rear with the R4 Jupiter in front. (*Thoroughbred & Classic Car magazine*)

JOWETT R.4 *JUPITER*

PROVISIONAL TECHNICAL DATA

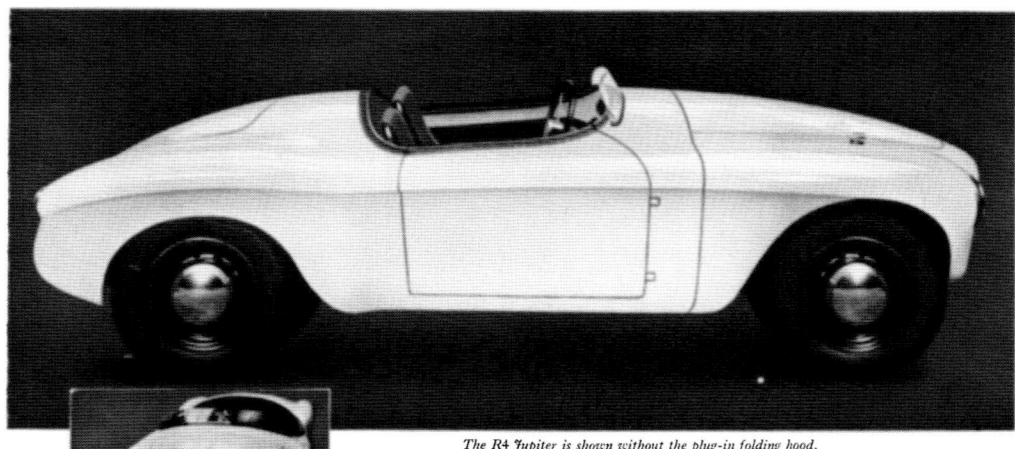

The R4 Jupiter is shown without the plug-in folding hood.

The designer of a high-speed car has a number of ideal requirements to incorporate into his vehicle, but amongst the most desirable are exceptional power to weight ratio, superlative road holding, steering and brakes, and a suspension system which allows the car's potential performance to be used on all manner of roads.

These qualities have been combined successfully and at a competitive price, in the Jowett R.4 Jupiter, a series development of the R.1 prototype which made such an impact by its racing successes.

Extremely modern and full of character, in styling the lines are simple and appealing to the connoisseur. Extensive use of laminated plastics has been made in the body. One advantage of the process used is the ease of repair, in addition to the advantages of strength, lightness and lower cost.

Road holding, braking, steering and road behaviour are exceptionally good due to the very rigid built-in chassis and welded steel bulkhead-structures. The performance is of a very high order thanks to the exceptionally good power to weight ratio.

The front cover of the four-page sales brochure for the R4 Jupiter.

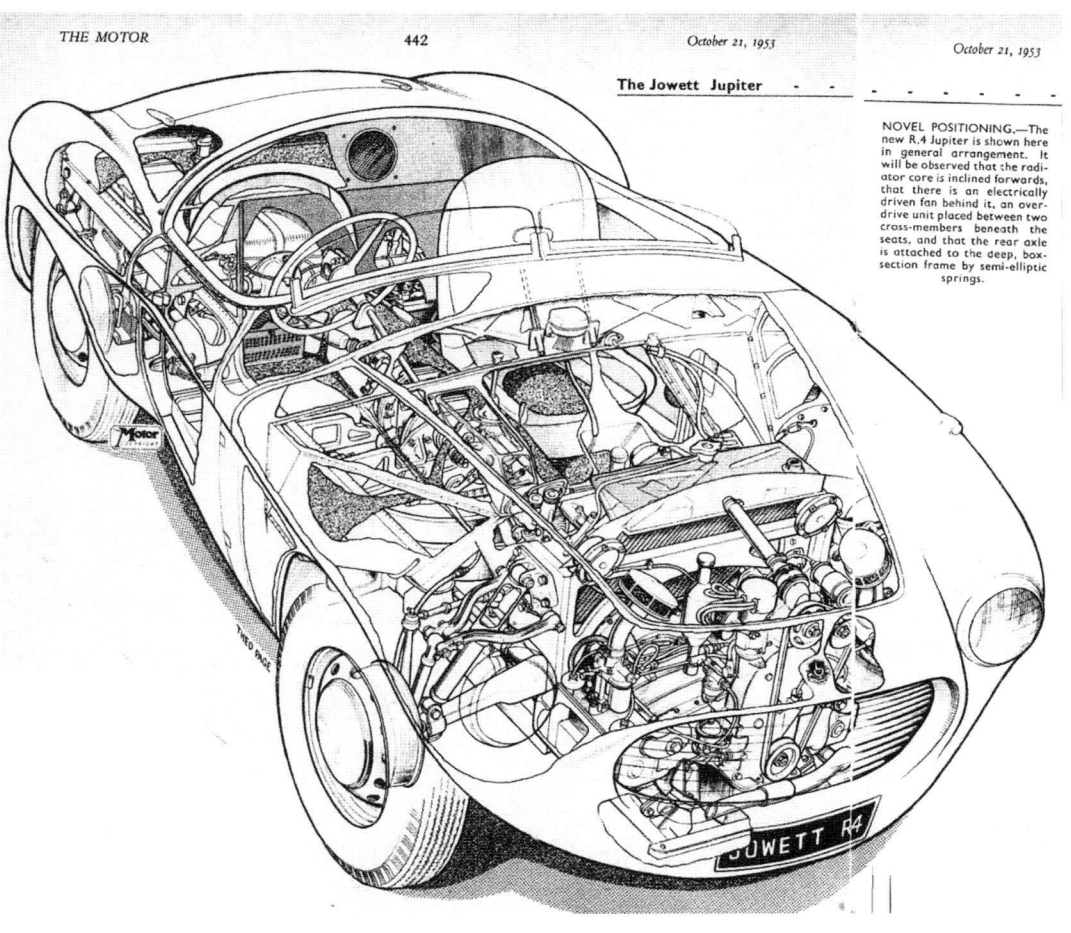

THE MOTOR   442   *October 21, 1953*   *October 21, 1953*

The Jowett Jupiter   -   -   -   -   -   -   -   -

NOVEL POSITIONING.—The new R.4 Jupiter is shown here in general arrangement. It will be observed that the radiator core is inclined forwards, that there is an electrically driven fan behind it, an over-drive unit placed between two cross-members beneath the seats, and that the rear axle is attached to the deep, box-section frame by semi-elliptic springs.

Cutaway line drawing of the R4 Jupiter. (*The Motor magazine*)

Two publicity shots of the R4 Jupiter. (*C. H. Wood*)

The famous Dutch rally driver, Maurice Gatsonides, enjoying a swift half at the wheel of a R4. He drove one of the R1 Jupiters in the 1952 Le Mans, but the car failed to finish.

Another period shot of the R4. (*JCC Archive*)

The R4 boarding the Silver City Airways plane in 1953, probably with Roy Lunn at the wheel on the car's testing and fact-finding trip to France. (*Silver City Airways*)

Opposite above: The R4 with the Mead and R1 Jupiters at the Jowett Car Club rally in 2005 in Basingstoke.

Opposite below: The R4 receiving some serious attention at the Jowett Car Club rally in Wakefield in 2010.

136

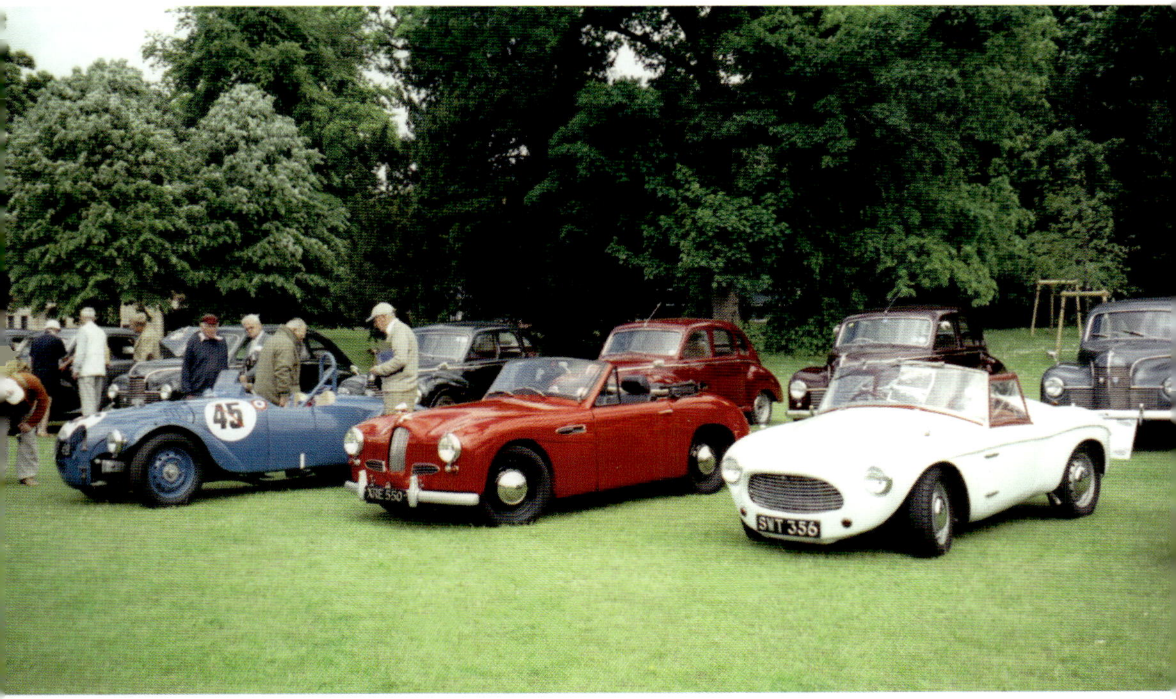
45
XRE 550
SWT 356

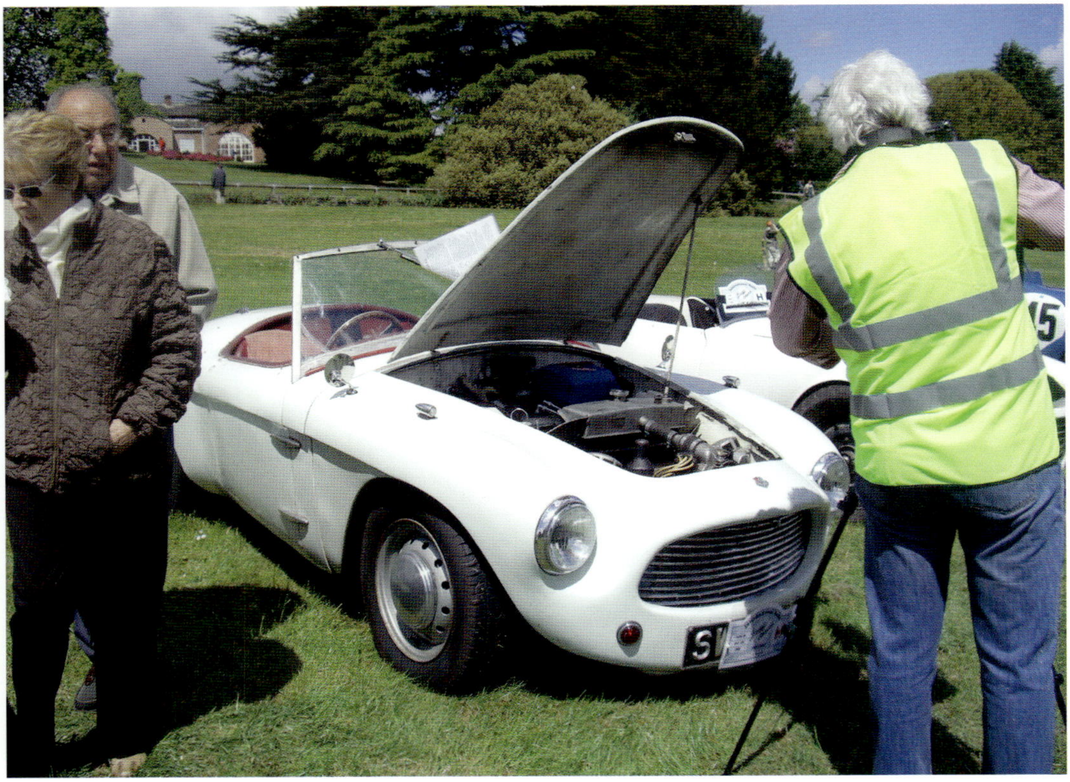

Another view of the R4 at the Jowett Car Club rally in Wakefield in 2010, the owner, Keith Patchett (*left*) with Phill Green (*right*) who helped build the car in Jowett's Experimental Department.

18

SOME MODERN REPLICAS

A S MENTIONED IN the text already, some examples of Jowett prototypes no longer survive, but over the years, several replicas have been built. Here are a selection of some of them.

This picture of a partially completed 1928 Sports Replica was being built by the late Ian Priestley, the club's pre-war registrar at the time of his untimely death in 2013. Several other replicas have been built; the following are some of them. (*I. Priestley*)

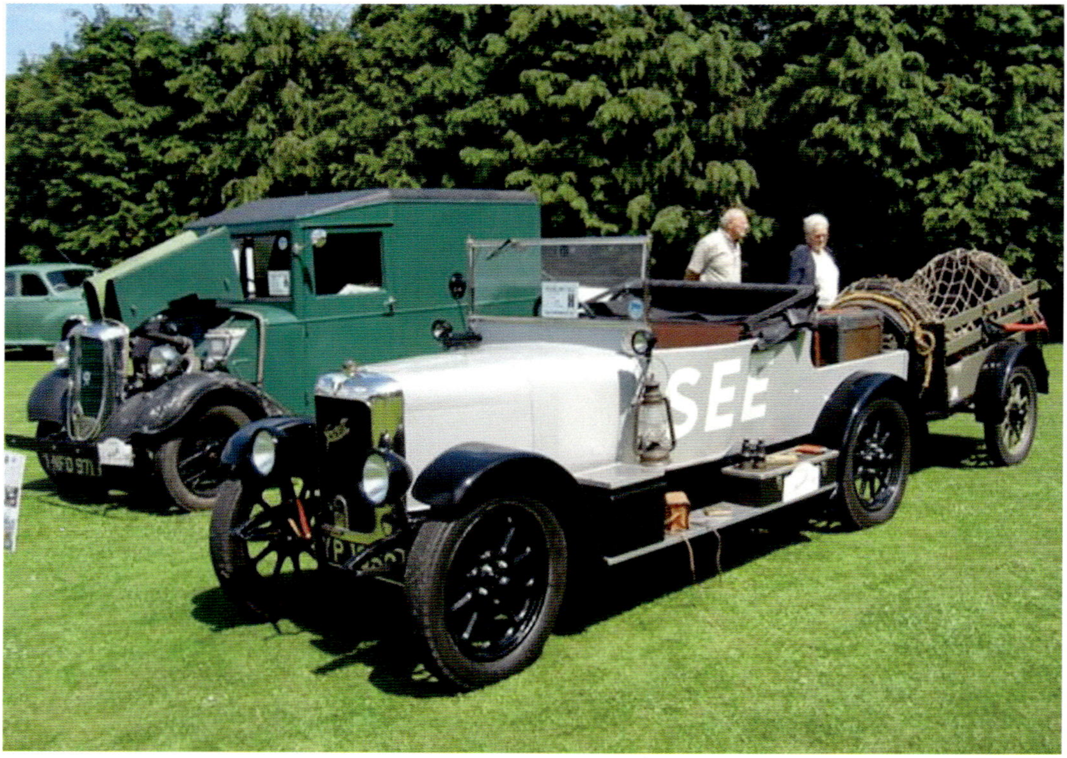

The See replica, an exact copy of the Wait & See cars of 1926, including the Eccles trailer filled with petrol cans, ropes, and other equipment taken on the original Africa crossing.

Two pictures of the replica of the Victoria Worsley Jowett Sports that was raced by her at various locations in 1928 and 1929, including Brooklands. This car was built by John Wilson in Australia. (*J. Wilson*)

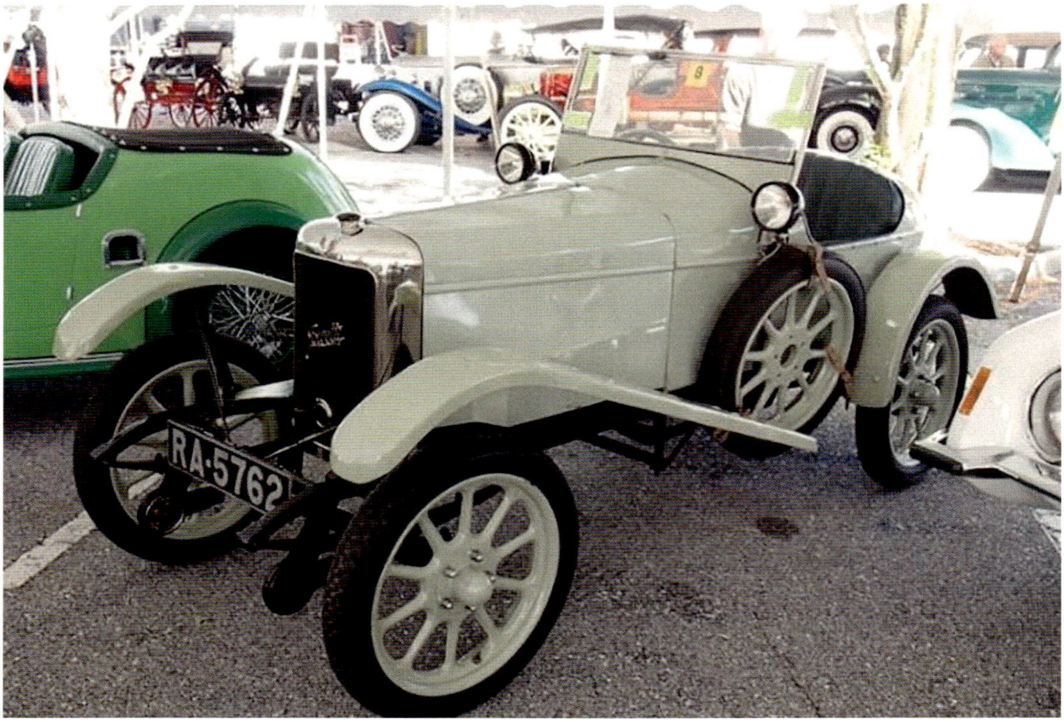
RA-5762

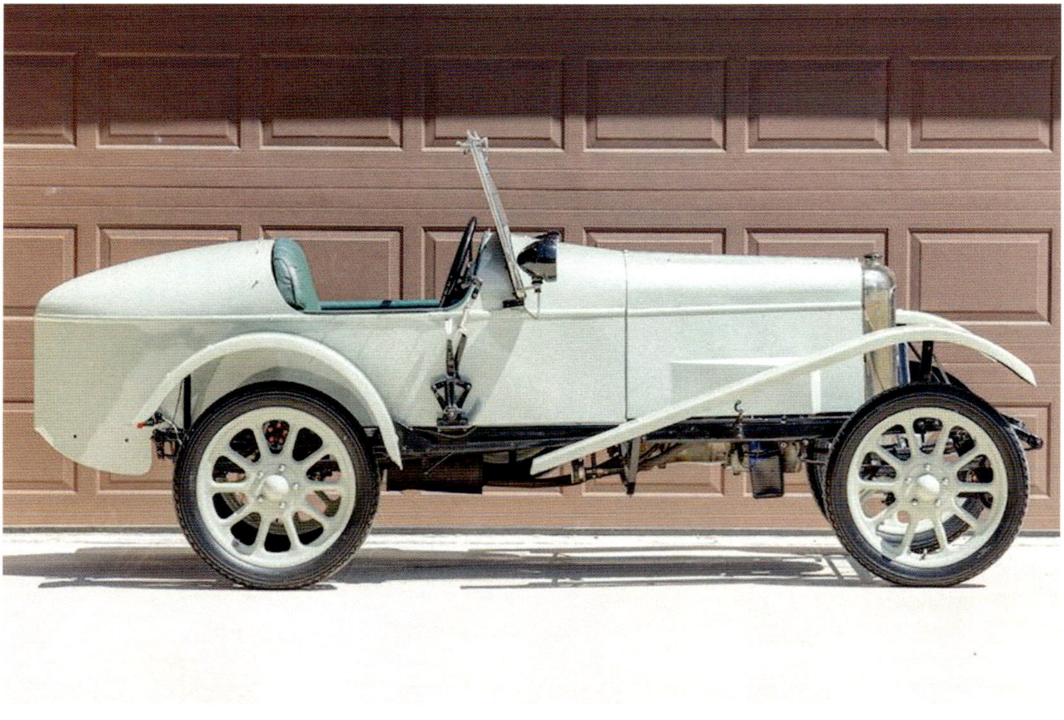

Opposite and above: Three pictures of the 1928 Brooklands twelve-hour record holder, which was driven by Horace Grimley of Jowett's Experimental Department and J. J. Hall, a professional record breaker who was based in Brooklands. This beautiful car was built by John Box, a club member, and was seen regularly in the 1980s and 1990s. It was later sold and exported to the USA; this is probably the only vintage Jowett in the States.

Above and below: Two pictures of *The Sand Racer*, which was rebuilt on a 1925 chassis. The car was said to have raced on the sands at Saltburn and Redcar in the 1920s, hence its name.

Above and below: Two pictures of another Jowett Sport built on a 1929 chassis known as *Polly*. This car is very active in VSCC trials. These pictures were taken at the Jowett Car Club rally in Llandridod Wells in 2012.

Above and below: In the chapter devoted to the 1928 Sports model, I also referred to the Jowett Coupé, which was also produced that year. I did not feature it as seventy were built during 1928 and 1929, yet sadly, none survive today. John Box built a close replica of one on a 1930 chassis, which he christened *The White Lady*.

Above and below: As mentioned in the CD Bradford chapter, four Utility examples came to New Zealand in 1953. One (CD2) was badly damaged in an accident with a lorry in 1955. It was repaired using a Zephyr front and bonnet. It was nearly scrapped in the early 1960s as the body was beyond restoration. It has been rebuilt with a home-built sports body using a Jupiter front, Morris Oxford MO doors, and Javelin rear wings. It is now known as CDR3. This reincarnation was carried out by Vic Morrison (pictured above), who still owns it and uses it regularly. (*V. Morrison*)

Above and below: This stunning replica of the 1951 Le Mans R1 Jupiter was built in Australia in 1998 by Fergus King. He obtained a wrecked Javelin saloon and removed the body, and after much mechanical work, fabricated the body which is in polished aluminium. It really is a stunning car and a real credit to him. (*F. King*)

Select Bibliography and Acknowledgements

Cotton, M., *The Design Realisation Unit 1942–1972*
Frostick, M., *The Cars That Got Away* (Cassell, 1968)
Goodway, D., *Herbert Read Reassessed* (Liverpool University Press, 1998)
Lord Montagu of Beaulieu, *Lost Causes of Motoring* (Cassell, 1960)
Clark, P. and Nankivell, E., *Jowett: The Complete History* (Haynes Publishing, 1991)
Palmer, G. and Balfour, C., *Auto-Architect* (Magna Press, 1998)
The History of the Traffic Department of the Metropolitan Police

By Jupiter! the Jupiter Owners' Auto Club magazine
Classic & Sportscar magazine
Classic Car Weekly newspaper
Flat Four, the Jowett Car Club of New Zealand magazine
Motor Sport magazine
Octane magazine
The Autocar magazine
The Javelin, the Jowett Car Club of Australia magazine
The Jowetteer, the Jowett Car Club magazine
The Motor magazine
Thoroughbred & Classic Cars magazine
Tractor & Machinery magazine
Veteran & Vintage magazine

I would like to take this opportunity to thank my wife, Jane, for her continued support in all my literary efforts relating to Jowett cars; it is greatly appreciated. I would also like to thank my three children, Jonathan, Jessica, and Ben, who have grown up with Jowetts over the last thirty-five years, and also my son-in-law, Liam, who has supported me in all things motoring. Also, to my grandchildren, Luke, Daisy, Oliver, Alexander, Jack, Thomas, and Charlie—all 'Jowett Juniors' whom I hope will take up the Jowett cause in the future. Thanks also to Alan Rushworth for his excellent research into the CD Bradford range and the late Mike Worthington-Williams, the motoring journalist. Last, but not least, to my many friends in the Jowett Car Club and also locally, who have helped me considerably keeping my cars on the road.

Also by the Same Author

Jowett 1901–1954 (Images of Motoring)
My Car was a Jowett
Jowett: Advertising the Marque
Sporting Jowetts
Jowett: A Century of Memories
Jowetts of the 1920s
Jowett Cars of the 1930s
Journeys Around Whitby
The Jowett Bradford: Jowett's Unsung Hero

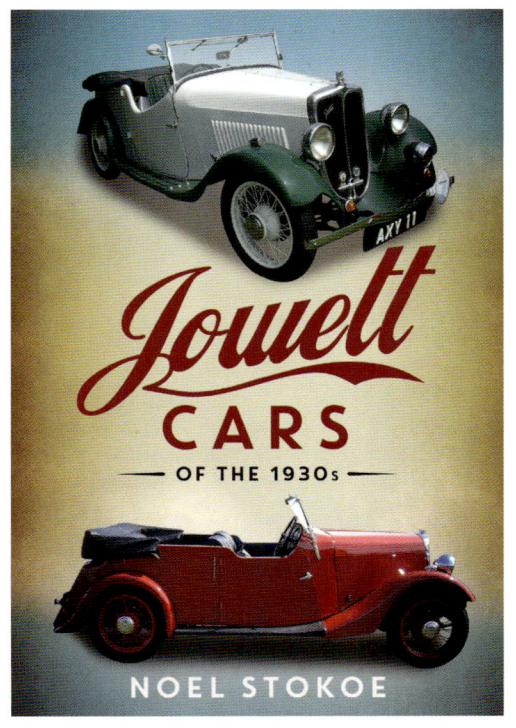